Collins

Cambridge Lower Secondary

English as a Second Language

STAGE 8: STUDENT'S BOOK

T0383297

Anna Osborn

Series Editor: Nick Coates

William Collins' dream of knowledge for all began with the publication of his first book in 1819.

A self-educated mill worker, he not only enriched millions of lives, but also founded a flourishing publishing house. Today, staying true to this spirit, Collins books are packed with inspiration, innovation and practical expertise.

They place you at the centre of a world of possibility and give you exactly what you need to explore it.

Collins. Freedom to teach.

Published by Collins
An imprint of HarperCollins*Publishers*
The News Building
1 London Bridge Street
London
SE1 9GF

HarperCollins*Publishers*
Macken House, 39/40 Mayor Street Upper,
Dublin 1, D01 C9W8, Ireland

Browse the complete Collins catalogue at
www.collins.co.uk

© HarperCollins*Publishers* Limited 2021

10 9 8 7

ISBN 978-0-00-836680-3

British Library Cataloguing-in-Publication Data
A catalogue record for this publication is available from the British Library.

Author: Anna Osborn
Series Editor: Nick Coates
Project manager: Lucy Hobbs
Development editor: Helen King
Product manager: Lucy Cooper
Proof-reader: Sue Chapple
Cover designer: Gordon MacGlip
Cover illustrator: Maria Herbert-Liew
Typesetter: Jouve India Private Ltd
Production controller: Lyndsey Rogers
Printed in India by Multivista Global Pvt. Ltd.

MIX
Paper | Supporting responsible forestry
FSC™ C007454
FSC
www.fsc.org

This book contains FSC™ certified paper and other controlled sources to ensure responsible forest management.

For more information visit: www.harpercollins.co.uk/green

Acknowledgements:

The publishers gratefully acknowledge the permission granted to reproduce the copyright material in this book. Every effort has been made to trace copyright holders and to obtain their permission for the use of copyright material. The publishers will gladly receive any information enabling them to rectify any error or omission at the first opportunity.

With thanks to the following teachers and schools for reviewing materials in development: Hawar International School; Khushnuma Gandhi, HVB Global Academy; Judith Hughes, International School of Budapest; Babara Khan, Jankidevi Public School.

Contents

Contents map   4

   Unit 1 Film and drama   7

   Unit 2 Being a good sport   17

Review 1   27

   Unit 3 School rules!   29

   Unit 4 Bookworms   39

Review 2   49

   Unit 5 Extreme weather   51

   Unit 6 Extreme planet   61

Review 3   71

   Unit 7 Back in time   73

   Unit 8 Who am I?   83

Mid-year review   93

   Unit 9 Power of music   99

 Unit 10 City life   109

Review 4   119

Unit 11 A job for life   121

Unit 12 Helping hand   131

Review 5   141

Unit 13 The digital generation   143

Unit 14 Advertising   153

Review 6   163

Unit 15 Great inventors   165

Unit 16 Robots and the future   175

End-of-year review   185

Key word list   191

Acknowledgements   198

Contents map

Unit / Topic	Reading	Listening	Speaking	Writing	Use of English
1 Film and drama	Film reviews and descriptions of people's film preferences	• A conversation about making plans to go to the cinema	• Discussion: films you like / don't like • Role play: making plans • Word stress on prefixes	• Two film reviews	• Verbs + –ing forms • Revision of present tenses • Revision of future tenses
Project: writing a scene from a play					
Focus on Drama: acting a scene of a play					
2 Being a good sport	• A questionnaire about being a good sport	• A conversation about an athlete	• Discussion: what is a good sport? • Discussion: an athlete you admire • Intonation in questions	• A fact file: an athlete you admire	• Comparing with adverbs • Revision of past tenses • Past perfect
Project: a sports survey					
Focus on the World: origins of sports					
Review 1					
3 School rules!	• An article about unusual schools	• A conversation about unusual schools • A podcast about unusual school journeys	• Discussion: is school important?	• An opinion essay: is school important?	• Present perfect (with ever, never, just, yet) • –ing form as a noun
Project: design your perfect school					
Focus on Social Studies: human rights					
4 Bookworms	• An article about an unusual library	• An interview about why reading is good for us	• Discussion: books, reading and libraries • Discussion: e-readers • Express disbelief and surprise	• A discussion essay: the advantages and disadvantages of e-readers	• Questions with prepositions • Connectives for contrast (although, though, while)
Project: make a Little Free Library					
Focus on Literature: what makes a good story? (Wisha Wozzariter by Payal Kapadia)					
Review 2					
5 Extreme weather	• A blog post about an extreme weather event • Text messages about the weather	• Weather forecasts	• Discussion: personal experiences of extreme weather	• A descriptive blog post: an extreme weather event	• Present simple and past simple passive • Adjectives with –ing and –ed endings • this, that, these and those
Project: a case study of an extreme weather event					
Focus on Geography: floods					
6 Extreme planet	• An article about extreme places on Earth	• A presentation about important animals	• Discussion: personal experiences of extreme places • Giving your opinion	• An opinion essay: what's the most important species?	• Adding information with relative clauses • Present continuous passive
Project: plan a world tour					
Focus on the World: extreme tour of the world					
Review 3					

Unit / Topic	Reading	Listening	Speaking	Writing	Use of English
7 Back in time	• Descriptions of unusual historical experiences	• Presentations from two historians about King Tutankhamun	• Discussion: your favourite time in history • Discussion: is history important? • Word stress in compound nouns	• A profile: an important person from history	• Compound nouns • Past perfect with *ever, never, always* and *already*
Project: make a time capsule					
Focus on History: archaeologists' greatest finds					
8 Who am I?	• Online forum posts about people's identity and character	• An interview with twins about identity	• Discussion: your identity and character • Checking what somebody said	• An email to a new pen pal telling them about yourself	• Prepositions after adjectives • Questions ending with prepositions • Reported speech
Project: make a display about your class – Who are we?					
Focus on Literature: non-fiction (*I Will Always Write Back* by Martin Ganda and Caitlin Alifirenka)					
Mid-year review					
9 Power of music	• A blog post about the power of music to change the world	• Short interviews with people talking about what music means to them	• Discussion: can music change the world? • Dealing with words you don't know • Discussion: you and music	• An opinion blog post: can music bring people together?	• Prepositions after verbs • Defining relative clauses • Reported questions
Project: your song					
Focus on Music: instrument families in an orchestra					
10 City life	• An article about what makes a great city	• A debate about city and country living	• Discussion: city or country living • Presentation: your favourite city	• A description of your favourite city	• Reported commands • to + verb after adjectives and verbs • Noun phrases
Project: design an ideal city					
Focus on the World: the best cities in the world					
Review 4					
11 A job for life	• An article about jobs that make people happy	• A podcast about jobs different students want to do	• Discussion: what you are looking for in a job • Explaining your opinion	• A description of your dream job	• Phrasal verbs with *put* • Polite questions • Modal verbs (*might, might not, may, may not, should, shouldn't, would, could*)
Project: a survey about jobs					
Focus on Maths: analysing data					

Unit / Topic	Reading	Listening	Speaking	Writing	Use of English
12 Helping hand	• An article about different charities	• A podcast about helping people	• Discussion: ways to help people • Presentation: talking about a charity	• A letter to your head teacher to persuade them to support a charity	• Modal verbs (*must, mustn't, have to, don't have to*) • Likely and unlikely conditionals • Indefinite pronouns (*anywhere, someone,* etc.)
Project: the kindness project					
Focus on Literature: what's the author's message? (*Wonder* by RJ Palacio)					
Review 5					
13 The digital generation	• A blog post about someone's relationship to their mobile phone	• A conversation between a mother and son about being addicted to technological devices	• Discussion: you and technology • Checking what somebody said • Discussion: growing up in the digital age	• A discussion essay: the advantages and disadvantages of growing up in the digital age	• *If only / wish that / should have / shouldn't have* for regrets • Abstract nouns • Multi-word verbs with *give*
Project: our digital footprint					
Focus on ICT: staying safe online					
14 Advertising	• Shop signs • A product review of a new phone	• A radio show about teenagers and advertising	• Discussion: how you like to shop • Discussion: advertising	• A product review	• Talking about quantity of uncountable items • Conjunctions of purpose (*so that, in order to, to*) • Compound adjectives
Project: make your own advertisement					
Focus on the World: publicity campaigns from around the world					
Review 6					
15 Great inventors	• An article about teenage inventors	• A podcast about important inventions	• Discussion: the best and worst inventions	• A story about an invention	• Relative clauses with prepositions • Verbs with *–ing* form and to + verb • Present perfect continuous
Project: make an inventions timeline					
Focus on Science: infectious diseases					
16 Robots and the future	• Online forum posts about what robots will be able to do in the future	• A conversation about robot workers	• Discussion: robots with intelligence • Intonation of tag questions	• An opinion essay: will robots control the world one day?	• Nouns and prepositions • Abstract nouns • Multi-word verbs with cut • Future passive
Project: design a new robot					
Focus on Literature: creating excitement in a story (Frankenstein by Mary Shelley)					
End-of year review					

Film and drama

1

Looking forward

This unit looks at films and what we think about them, and provides an opportunity to write some original drama.

You will read

- film reviews
- a scene from a play

You will listen

- to people making plans to go to the cinema

You will speak

- about films that you like / don't like
- about making a plan to watch a film
- in character, in a scene of a play

You will write

- two film reviews
- a scene of a play

You will learn

- to use verbs + –*ing* forms
- to use a range of present tenses
- to use a range of future tenses

Choosing a film

Discuss in groups.

- What sort of films do you like / not like and why?
- Where do you like to watch films?
- Who do you watch films with?
- What's the best film you've ever seen? What was it about? Why did you like it so much?
- What do you think makes a film good or bad?

Vocabulary: types of film

1 **Look and match the types of film to the pictures.**

comedy   musical   animated film   science fiction   documentary   drama

2 **Rank the types of film by how much you like them from 1 (you like most) to 6 (you like least). Be prepared to give reasons for your point of view.**

Reading: film reviews

1 **Discuss.**

- What are film reviews and where do you usually find them?
- What sort of information about a film would you expect to see in a film review?
- Do you read / follow recommendations given in film reviews? Why? / Why not?
- Would you like to have a job writing film reviews? Why? / Why not?

explain and justify your point of view; talk about film reviews

2 Match the people (1–3) to the films (A–E).

1 Ryan loves watching films about sport. He hates going to see animated films and musicals because he thinks that those sorts of films are just for children.

2 Simon likes watching funny films about real people and loved the film *Old Hat* last year. His friend suggested going to watch the sequel, but Simon usually avoids watching sequels unless they get very good reviews. He would rather watch a good, new film than a bad sequel.

3 Marta doesn't mind watching historical dramas but she really enjoys going to see films that are set in the future. She particularly likes stories that are set in space.

FILM REVIEWS

A Sweet Fun ★ ☆ ☆ ☆ ☆

People say that real life is funnier than fiction. This is definitely true of the new comedy *Sweet Fun*, from director Giuseppe Palma. It's a true story about a group of people working in a kitchen. Fun and easy to watch.

C More Old Hat ☆ ☆ ☆ ☆ ☆

More Old Hat, the sequel to the excellent comedy *Old Hat*, is about a woman in New York who makes her own clothes. Unfortunately, the sequel is not as good as the original film. The sets are still good, but the plot is unrealistic and the jokes are unoriginal. Disappointing.

E Tom's Dream ★ ★ ★ ★ ☆

A new historical drama from writer Harriet Parks, *Tom's Dream* is about a young boy in the 1950s, who dreams of being a professional athlete. He practises running around his local park every day, until he's good enough to join a team. The acting is excellent and Kieran Harris is particularly good as the main character.

B Mouse on Goal ★ ★ ★ ★ ☆

Who says animated films are just for kids?! *Mouse on Goal* is both funny and clever. It's about a singing mouse from Madrid, who happens to be a professional footballer! "I'm singing while I'm scoring a goal," is my favourite line from the film! The actors who give the mice their voices are brilliant and the script is fantastic.

D Don't Look Back ★ ★ ★ ★ ★

This amazing new science-fiction film is set in the year 2150 and tells the story of a group of astronauts who can't get back to Earth. The special effects are quite extraordinary and the characters are very realistic. Recommended for sci-fi fans.

Vocabulary: talking about films

Look at the words from the reviews, then copy and complete the table.

unoriginal   acting   main character   director   unrealistic   special effects
disappointing   extraordinary   plot   realistic   script   actor   original
sequel   sets   writer

A: People who make or are in films	B: Other nouns used to talk about films	C: Adjectives used to describe films

Speaking: word stress on prefixes, for contrast

1 (1A) **Listen and mark the word stress of the words in bold. What part of the antonym do we stress?**

Sarah: I think the plot was very **original** and the acting was very **realistic**.

Pierre: Oh, I disagree. I think the plot was completely **unoriginal** and the acting was totally **unrealistic**.

2 **Which of the films on page 9 would you / wouldn't you like to see and why? Use the words in *Vocabulary: talking about films* and the correct word stress.**

Use of English: verbs + –*ing* forms

1 **Copy and complete these sentences.**

*Ryan **loves** [1]...... (watch) films about sport. He **hates** [2]...... (go) to see animated films and musicals.*

2 **What do you do to the verbs that come after *love* and *hate*?**

a add –*s*   b add –*ing*   c add –*ed*

3 **Find another five verbs on page 9 that follow the same rule.**

Use of English: revision of present tenses

1 Match the tenses in the box to the examples from the text on page 9.

> present simple   present continuous

1 *"People say that real life is funnier than fiction."*

2 *"He practises running around his local park every day…"*

3 *"In fact, animated films are becoming more and more original."*

4 *"I'm singing while I'm scoring a goal!"*

2 Copy and match the rules with the examples from Activity 1.

a We use the present simple to talk about something we do regularly.

b We use the present simple to talk about general truths.

c We use the present continuous to talk about things we're doing now.

d We use the present continuous to talk about trends or changes that are happening around now.

3 Discuss, using the correct present tense.

1 What are you doing at the moment?

2 What do you do after school on Wednesdays?

3 Tell your partner one fact about the planet.

4 Talk about changes in the world's climate at the moment.

Writing: film reviews

1 Read the instructions and make notes.

You are going to write two film reviews, one about a film you enjoyed and one about a film you didn't enjoy.

1 What two films are you going to write about?

2 What words from **Vocabulary: talking about films** on page 10 can you use in your reviews?

2 Plan your two film reviews.

Look again at the reviews on page 9. Put the questions below in the order that they are answered in each review.

a What's it about and where / when is it set?

b What's the title of the film?

c What's your opinion of the film and would you recommend it?

d What type of film is it?

Now write two plans for your two film reviews by answering the questions in the correct order. Remember not to tell people too much about the plot of the film and definitely not the ending!

3 Write your two film reviews. *Don't* write the titles of the films in the reviews.

4 Read your work and ask yourself the following questions.

* *Have I checked for any missing words?*

* *Have I checked my spelling and punctuation?*

5 Share your review with a partner.

Read your partner's reviews.

1 Which film did they enjoy and which didn't they enjoy? How do you know?

2 Can you guess the titles of the films they have written about?

use a range of present tenses; generate ideas, plan and draft a review **11**

Making plans to see a film

Listening: which film shall we go to see?

1 🔊 **1B** **Listen and choose the correct picture.**

1 What film are the boys going to watch?

a    b    c

2 What time does the film start?

a    b    c

2 🔊 **1B** **Listen again and decide if it is Tom, Chris or Lionel who:**

1 suggests going to the cinema tomorrow. *Lionel*

2 is going to visit his grandparents this weekend.

3 doesn't like sci-fi films.

4 is playing football tomorrow.

5 is going to buy both tickets for the cinema today.

6 is going to bring some snacks.

Speaking: making plans

1 **Match the phrases with the uses.**

1 "Sorry, I have plans on Saturday."

2 "Shall we go to the cinema?"

3 "Are you busy / free on Saturday?"

4 "Good idea. That would be fun!"

5 "Yes, I'm free on Saturday."

a to find out if someone is free

b to say you're free

c to say you're busy

d to make a suggestion

e to respond positively to a suggestion

2 🔊 **1C** **Listen and repeat the phrases with the correct intonation.**

3 **Work in groups of three to complete a role play. Then swap roles so that everyone plays each role.**

Student A: You are looking for someone to go to the cinema with tomorrow. Ask Student B, then Student C. Then make a plan.

Student B: You are busy tomorrow. Listen and respond to Student A.

Student C: You are free tomorrow. Listen and respond to Student A. Then make a plan.

listen for specific information; make links in response to what others say

Use of English: revision of future forms

1 **Look and match the examples to the situations.**

1 *I'm going to spend the weekend with my grandparents.*

2 *We're having a birthday party for my grandmother on Sunday.*

3 *Shall we go to the cinema in the afternoon?*

4 *I've read a lot of disappointing reviews, so I don't think it's going to be very good.*

5 *OK. I don't know anything about it, but I think it'll be fun!*

6 *The afternoon film starts at 3 o'clock.*

7 *Will you buy my ticket too?*

8 *I'll pay you back tomorrow.*

9 *Shall I bring some snacks tomorrow?*

a   a prediction without evidence

b   a request asking someone to do something

c   a promise to do something

d   a suggestion to do something

e   an offer to do something

f   a prediction with evidence

g   a plan, not always arranged

h   a fixed plan arranged with other people

i   a scheduled event

2 **Copy and complete the grammar rules with the words from the box.**

going to + verb   present simple

present continuous   ~~will + verb~~   *shall* + verb

FUTURE FORMS AND USE

1   We use *will* + verb for predictions without evidence, requests and promises (a, b and c).

2   We use ____ for suggestions and offers (d and e).

3   We use ____ for predictions with evidence and plans (f and g).

4   We use the ____ for fixed plans (h).

5   We use the ____ for scheduled events (i).

> **Language tip**
>
> Sometimes more than one future form can be used in the same situation:
>
> *I'm travelling to London tomorrow.*
>
> *I'm going to travel to London tomorrow.*

3 **Discuss. Remember to use the correct future form.**

- What are you going to do this weekend?
- When do you next have plans with your friends? What are you doing?
- What do you think the planet will be like in 2100?
- What time does school start tomorrow?
- Make a promise to your partner about something you will do.
- Make a suggestion to your partner about something you could do this weekend.

Focus on Drama

Acting a scene from a play

1 Look at the play script and find these words and phrases. What do they mean?

> list of characters   act (n)   scene   (stage directions)

2 🔊 Work in groups of four. Listen to and read the script and discuss the questions in the OVER TO YOU boxes.

3 Prepare to act out the scene.

- First, practise by saying this line from the play aloud.

I just saw something.

- Say the same line in six different ways, following the stage directions.

> (in a frightened way)   (in a silly way, joking)   (trying to be brave)
>
> (with wonder)   (in a shy or nervous way)   (in a confident way)

- Now, act out the scene. Think about what your character is like and follow the stage directions carefully.

STEP BY WICKED STEP *by Anne Fine*

List of characters

RALPH *Clever, confident and sensible; a natural leader.*

CLAUDIA *Shy, quiet; thinks about others' feelings.*

PIXIE *Brave and confident.*

COLIN *Nervous; seems to be thinking about something else.*

ACT ONE

Scene one

A wild storm. We are at the top of a big old house. Two boys and two girls with travel bags are walking into a room through the dark, lit only by flashes of lightning.

CLAUDIA: Scary!

RALPH: (*joking*) What, scarier than that drive through the dark and the wet (*putting his fingers over her face*), with all the tree branches trying to get us?

PIXIE: And the lightning, which frightened Mr Plumley so much he almost missed the road and drove us into a hole?

OVER TO YOU

1 Who do you think will be the most interesting character?

2 Which character do you think will be most like you?

OVER TO YOU

1 How do you think the children are feeling and why?

2 How would you feel if you were there?

3 What do you think is going to happen in the first part of the scene?

RALPH: And that long ride up the drive covered in trees, past the little old church and into that strange yard full of shadows?

PIXIE: And the huge door that made such a loud noise when we pushed it open?

RALPH: Creeeeeeaaaaaak!

COLIN: (*amazed*) And that huge empty hall!

PIXIE: With all those cold, hard faces looking down at us.

CLAUDIA: (*trying to be brave*) They were just paintings.

RALPH: The famous Harwicks. Generations of them looking down at us with their cruel eyes.

PIXIE: (*as if she is one of the Harwicks*) School children! Horrible school children on a horrible school trip. Staying in our great house. For a whole week!

RALPH: (*as if he is one of the Harwicks*) Pulling their cheap little bags across our clean floors.

PIXIE: Walking up the big stairs.

RALPH: Then the next stairs after that, then the stairs after that. Step by step.

PIXIE: All frightened by our eyes.

RALPH: Frightened by the light of the moon!

PIXIE: Frightened by the sounds of their own feet.

CLAUDIA: And the spiders!

(*A huge flash of lightning and some thunder.*)

CLAUDIA: (*screams*) Aaah! That flash of lightning was right above us.

RALPH: (*in his own voice*) It almost came through the window. Colin? Colin?

COLIN: I just saw something.

CLAUDIA: Not rats!

COLIN: No, no. Just a line. Down that wall. There, in the lightning for a moment, it looked really strange. As if …

CLAUDIA: As if …?

COLIN: As if it might have been a door.

PIXIE: In *that* wall? Don't be silly!

COLIN: Wait, then. Wait for the next flash of lightning, then you'll see.

PIXIE: What, just sit here for …

(*Another huge flash and bang.*)

COLIN: See?

PIXIE: No.

CLAUDIA: I did, though. Colin's right. There is a line down the wall. (*she moves her finger over the wall*) There.

COLIN: And another across. (*he shows them*) Here.

OVER TO YOU

1 What do you think the children are going to do?

2 What do you think they might find if they go through the door?

3 What would you do if you were them?

CLAUDIA: A hidden door.

PIXIE: There must be a way to open it. Quick, feel round the edges and see if … There! You've done it!

(*The door in the wall opens to show a Victorian bedroom covered in dust. It looks like a room that hasn't been touched for many years.*)

CLAUDIA: Look at it!

COLIN: Don't go in!

RALPH: Why not?

COLIN: It's secret, isn't it? And private. Totally private. I mean, look at the spiders' webs. Surely nobody has been in here for years and years.

RALPH: Look at that bed.

CLAUDIA: (*touching it*) Covered in dust.

PIXIE: Everything is.

COLIN: (*touches something that makes a noise*)

PIXIE: (*turning quickly*) What's that? Oh, it's you. I thought it was …

RALPH: Who? The owner? Back in his room after a hundred years?

PIXIE: That long?

RALPH: Look round you, Pixie. Even my great grandmother's bedroom was more modern than this.

CLAUDIA: (*picks up a toy from the floor*) See this? A little hand-made wooden cow. Its leg is broken.

PIXIE: He was going to fix it.

RALPH: What makes you think he was a he?

PIXIE: This. (*picks a diary off the desk and blows off dust*) See? 'Richard Clayton Harwick. This is my story. Read it and cry.'

OVER TO YOU

1 What do you think will happen next?

2 What do you think Richard Clayton's story will be about?

3 What did you like / not like about this scene? Why?

Project: writing a scene of a play

What happens next? You are going to write the next scene of the play _Step by Wicked Step_ in groups of four.

1 **Brainstorm your ideas.**

- When are you going to set your scene? Are you going to continue the story with the four children in the house or jump back in time and explore Richard's story?
- Who is going to be in your scene?
- Where is it going to be set?
- What's going to happen?

2 **Plan your scene.**

A story arc can help you to plan your scene. Look at the story arc for the scene that you read on pages 14–15. Write your own story arc for your next scene.

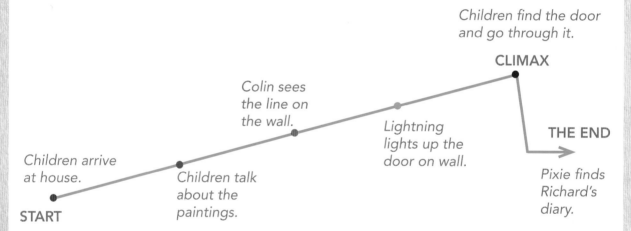

Children find the door and go through it.

CLIMAX

Colin sees the line on the wall.

Lightning lights up the door on wall.

THE END

Children arrive at house.

Children talk about the paintings.

START

Pixie finds Richard's diary.

3 **Write a first draft.**

- Write your script together as a group.
- You could write a character part each or you could write different sections of the scene as in your story arc.
- Don't forget stage directions.

4 **Read your scene aloud all the way through. Edit the script and make corrections.**

5 **Act out your scene.**

6 **Share with the class.**

Watch other students' scenes and give them some positive feedback about their script.

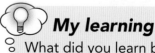

My learning

What did you learn by doing this project?

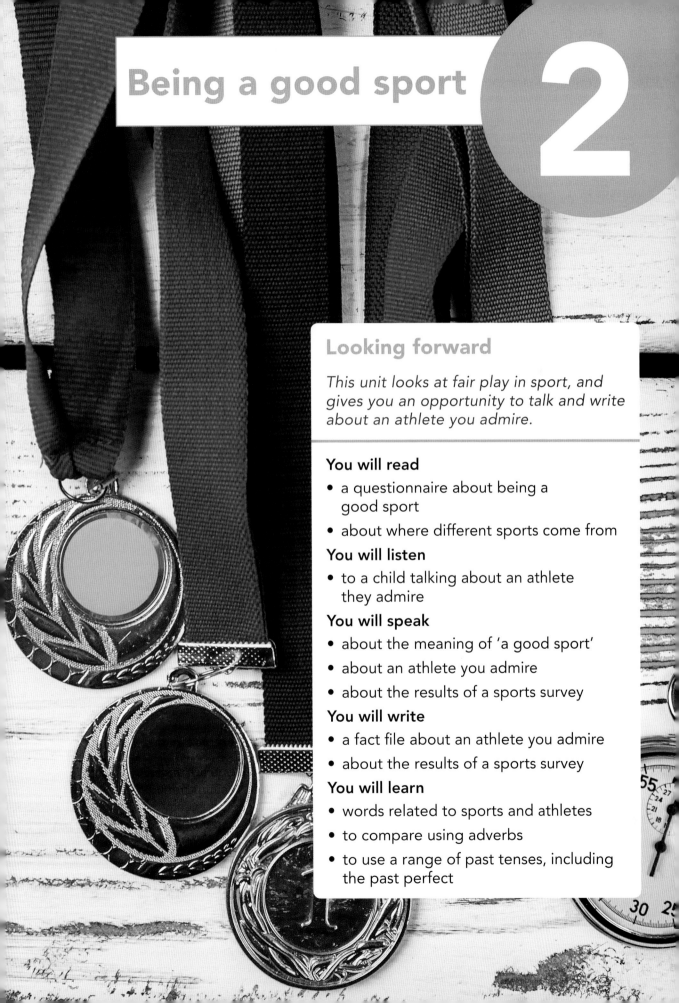

Being a good sport

2

Looking forward

This unit looks at fair play in sport, and gives you an opportunity to talk and write about an athlete you admire.

You will read
- a questionnaire about being a good sport
- about where different sports come from

You will listen
- to a child talking about an athlete they admire

You will speak
- about the meaning of 'a good sport'
- about an athlete you admire
- about the results of a sports survey

You will write
- a fact file about an athlete you admire
- about the results of a sports survey

You will learn
- words related to sports and athletes
- to compare using adverbs
- to use a range of past tenses, including the past perfect

Are you a good sport?

*A **good sport** is a person who plays fairly. They believe that doing their best is just as important as winning.*

Discuss.

1   What might a person who *is* a good sport do while playing in a match or competition?

2   What might a person who *isn't* a good sport do while playing in a match or competition?

3   Are you a good sport?

4   Do you prefer playing games or matches with people who are good sports? Why? / Why not?

5   Which of these people are good sports?

a *Sarah always follows the rules, even if it isn't to her advantage.*	**b** *Ricardo gets angry if his team loses and always blames his teammates.*
c *The only thing Marta cares about is winning the game, she doesn't care what she has to do.*	**d** *Jan always puts the team first, even if it means he doesn't score a goal himself.*

6   Rewrite sentences from question 5 so that all the people are good sports.

Vocabulary: revision of sports

1   Copy and complete the word webs.

basketball   opponent   hockey   rugby   referee   coach   volleyball
karate   player   golf

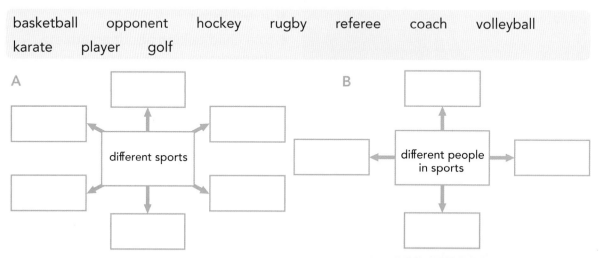

A — different sports

B — different people in sports

2   Discuss.

- Do you play or watch any of the sports from A above? Which is your favourite and why?
- Are there any other sports you like to play or watch? Why do you enjoy them?
- What do the people in B do in sport?

Language tip

A *match* or *game* is a competition between two teams or individual players.

A *tournament* is a competition between a number of teams or individual players.

A *championship* is a competition to decide who is the best player or team in a particular sport.

1 Read and complete the questionnaire for yourself. Then compare your answers with another student.

How good a sport are you?

To find out, choose **a**, **b** or **c** to complete these sentences

1 Your team wins a local tournament, so you …

   a celebrate and tell your opponents, "we play much better than you play".

   b celebrate with your team and forget about your opponents.

   c celebrate with your team and shake hands with your opponents.

2 The referee of a match you are playing in makes a decision that you think is wrong. You …

   a argue with the referee and accuse your opponents of cheating.

   b feel frustrated but try not to show it.

   c respect the referee's decision and carry on with the game.

3 Your volleyball coach takes you out of a match to give you some instructions. You …

   a sulk because you're playing well, and you want to get back to the game and beat your opponents.

   b feel frustrated but try not to show it.

   c listen carefully so that you can play slightly better than you did before.

4 You think that winning is …

   a much more important than taking part.

   b just as important as taking part.

   c not as important as taking part.

2 Now find out your results! Copy and complete the answers with phrases from the box.

> you're trying to be a good sport   you're a really good sport   you're not a good sport

If you scored:

mostly **a**, then [1]_____! Try to play by the rules or you may end up playing all by yourself!

mostly **b**, then [2]_____! You know how you should behave, but you sometimes forget to do it.
  Try to remember next time you're playing a game!

mostly **c**, then [3]_____! Keep doing what you're doing and you'll always play the best. Everyone will want you on their team!

Vocabulary: sports verbs

1 Do these verbs have a positive or negative meaning?

celebrate   sulk   congratulate   argue   respect   cheat

2 Write the correct form of the missing verbs from Activity 1 in your notebook.

When I was younger, I didn't use to be a very good sport. I never used to ¹*respect* the referee and sometimes I used to ²_____ with him. If we didn't win, I used to ³_____ in a corner. However, once, during a game of football, I scored a goal with my hand. The referee gave us the goal and we won the game 2–1. At the end, one of the opponents ⁴_____ me. I felt bad. We hadn't really won the game, because I had ⁵_____. I told the referee what had happened and he changed the result to a 1–1 draw. We all ⁶_____ together!

Use of English: comparing using adverbs

1 Look at these sentences from the questionnaire and the answers on page 19. Copy and complete the table, writing the adverbs in the correct place.

We play better *than you play.*

You sulk because you're playing well *and you want to get back to the game.*

You'll always play the best.

adverb	comparative adverb	superlative adverb
1_____	2_____	3_____

2 Read these sentences which compare how quickly some girls run. Write the girls' names in a line to show the order from slowest to quickest.

Laura and Misha run slightly more quickly *than Jane.*

Saira runs much more quickly *than Laura and Misha.*

Laura runs just as quickly *as Misha.*

Jane doesn't run as quickly as Laura and Misha.

the slowest   the quickest

1_____   2_____ / 3_____   4_____

3 Work in groups of three. Compare yourselves using the words in the box and the structures from activities 1 and 2.

ride a bike well / badly   speak quickly / slowly   sing loudly / quietly

I ride a bike slightly better than Ahmed. Kamil rides a bike the best.

An athlete you admire

Read and match the words in italics to the correct definitions.

> I really [1]*admire* [2]*professional* [3]*athletes* who take part in [4]*triathlons*. I think a [5]*gold medal* or a [6]*silver medal* or a [7]*bronze medal* are all really big [8]*achievements* in this sport.

a   a prize you get for coming second in a sports competition

b   an individual race in which you have to do three different sports

c   a prize you get for coming first in a sports competition

d   doing something for money rather than just for fun

e   something you have succeeded in doing, especially if you've tried very hard to do it

f   a prize you get for coming third in a sports competition

g   like and respect someone or something very much

h   a person who is good at a team or individual sport

Listening: an athlete I admire

1 (2A) **Listen once. Which sports are mentioned?**

2 (2A) **Copy the fact file. Then listen again and complete it.**

AN ATHLETE I ADMIRE	
Name	1 _____
Date of birth	2 _____
Nationality	3 _____
Sport	4 _____
First big sporting achievement	5 _____
Greatest sporting achievement	6 _____

3 **Discuss.**

I admire him because of a race he didn't win.

- Why does Dylan admire Alistair because of a race he didn't win?
- Do you agree with Dylan on this? Is it more important to be a good sport than to win the gold medal?
- Would you have helped your brother or sister, or a friend?
- Would you have helped a person you didn't know?
- Have you ever been helped by someone when playing sports?

> **Skills tip**
>
> When you're writing a fact file, you can make notes. You don't need to write full sentences.

Speaking: intonation in questions

1 **(2A)** **Listen to these questions from the conversation. At the end of each question, does the intonation go up (rising intonation) or does it go down (falling intonation)?**

1 Have you heard of him?

2 Is that why you chose him?

3 What sports does he play?

4 Why was that race special?

2 **Which type of questions use rising intonation? Which type of questions generally use falling intonation?**

3 **Say these questions using the correct intonation.**

1 What's your favourite sport?

2 Do you play often?

3 Where do you play?

4 Is it difficult to learn?

Vocabulary: sports adjectives

Discuss.

- Which professional athletes do you admire and why?
- What adjectives would you use to describe professional athletes?

strong

hard-working

lazy

competitive

unfit

Use of English: revision of past tenses

1 **Match the tenses to the examples.**

past simple   past continuous   present perfect   *used to* + infinitive

1 *I've decided to write about Alistair Brownlee.*

2 *He used to do cross-country running when he was young.*

3 *He won gold medals in 2012 and 2016.*

4 *… when Alistair was running past, …*

2 **Copy and complete the rules with the tenses from Activity 1.**

1 We use the _____ to talk about an action in the past that has an effect on the present.

2 We use the _____ to talk about completed actions in the past.

3 We use the _____ to talk about something that was happening over a period of time in the past.

4 We use _____ to talk about repeated actions in the past.

3 **Answer the questions using the correct past tense.**

1 What were you doing at three o'clock yesterday?

2 What did you do last Saturday?

3 What did you use to do after school when you were nine?

4 Have you ever done a triathlon?

Use of English: past perfect

1 **Look at this sentence from the listening on page 21. The underlined verb is in the past perfect tense. Answer the questions.**

After Chris <u>had finished</u> the first term, he decided to study Sports Science instead.

1 How is the past perfect tense formed?

2 What happened first – finishing the first term or deciding to study Sports Science?

3 Is the past perfect used to talk about a time before an action or event in the past or in the future?

Note that we often use the past perfect with other words including *before* and *when*.

Chris decided to study Sports Science before he <u>had finished</u> the first term.

When Chris <u>had finished</u> the first term, he decided to study Sports Science.

2 **Talk about things you *had* done.**

> What had you done before you arrived at school today?

> I had eaten breakfast.
>
> I had finished my homework.

Writing: a fact file

1 **Look at the fact file on page 21 and choose the correct options.**

1 A fact file includes …

   a important facts and figures.   b detailed explanations.

2 We use …

   a notes.   b full sentences.

3 A fact file is usually set in …

   a paragraphs.   b a table with columns and rows.

2 **Copy and complete the fact file on page 21 about an athlete you admire.**

3 **Complete this sentence with one or two reasons to explain your opinion.**

I admire this athlete because …

4 **Compare.**

Show your fact file to another student and compare the athletes. Use the expressions below.

just as … as   not as … as   much … than   slightly … than

Focus on the World

Origins of sports

1 Where do you think these sports were first played? Match the places in the box to the pictures.

| USA | England | Ancient Greece | France | China |

1
2
3
4
5

2 Read and check your answers to Activity 1.

Where do sports come from?

When you play a sport, do you ever think about who first came up with the idea for it? Who made the rules? Where was it first played?

Sport first became an important part of everyday life in Ancient Greece. The first Olympic Games took place in 776 BCE, in Olympia in Greece. At the beginning, this used to be just a one-day athletics event, with running races. Later, in the seventh century BCE, other events were added, including long jump and throwing.

The very first football matches were played in China in the third century BCE. Soldiers used to play football as exercise. The ball that they used was smaller than the balls used today (only 30–40 cm wide), and it was made of leather and filled with animal hair.

Tennis was first played in France in around 1000 CE. People used to shout the word *tenez*, which is the French word for *to take*, when they started playing. It became more and more popular, and by the fifteenth century, there were said to be many tennis courts in France.

Rugby was first played in England. The boys at Rugby School used to play a different kind of football, where they were allowed to catch the ball and kick it out of their hands. In 1823, a student called William Ellis was playing this game of Rugby School football when he picked up the ball and started to run with it. This was how running with the ball in rugby began!

Basketball is one of the newest sports that we play today. It was first played in the USA in 1892. It was invented by a Canadian doctor who was called James Naismith. He was looking for a game that could be played indoors during the cold winter months. It is said that he wrote the rules of basketball in about half an hour and most are still true of the game today. Some rules have changed, however. For example, in the original game players weren't allowed to bounce the ball.

3 **Write down the missing information in your notebook. You have one minute to find the answers in the text!**

1 The first Olympic Games took place in _____ .
2 The first footballs were _____ wide.
3 People first played tennis in France in _____ .
4 The game of rugby was first played in _____ .
5 The rules of basketball were written in _____ .

Language tip

BCE is short for Before Common Era.

When we say the seventh century, we mean the years from 601 to 699 BCE.

4 **Answer the questions.**

1 What sports were played at the first Olympic Games?
2 Who were the first football players and why did they play?
3 Where did the word *tennis* come from?
4 How did running with the ball in rugby start?
5 Why did James Naismith invent basketball?

5 **Find forms of the words in the text. Then rewrite the sentences, replacing the underlined sections with the correct form of the words.**

be allowed to (v)   indoors (adv)   invent (v)   original (adj)   bounce (v)

1 It was raining so we played inside the building.
2 I was the first person to think of this machine.
3 We followed the earliest rules.
4 The boys have permission to run in the race.
5 The ball hit the ground and immediately moved away from it again before it crossed the net.

6 **Research and discuss.**

Choose a sport that hasn't been talked about in the text and find out about where it was first played. Write down two interesting facts about its history. Compare your findings with another student.

Project: a sports survey

How sporty are we?

You are going to do a class survey about sports.

1. **Copy and complete the questions.**

   1 _____ your favourite sport to play?
   2 What's your favourite sport _____ watch?
   3 How _____ times a week do you play sport? Give details.
   4 _____ many minutes a week do you spend playing sport? Give details.
   5 _____ you a member of a sports club? Give details.
   6 _____ you take part in sports competitions? Give details.

2. **Ask five students the questions from Activity 1 and make notes of their answers.**

3. **Talk to another student and compare your results. Did you get the same results or were they different?**

4. **Put your results together. Copy and complete the results table. What conclusions can you make from your results? Do you think your class plays enough sport? Why? / Why not?**

Our sports survey results	
Number of students questioned	10
Most popular sport to play	
Most popular sport to watch	
Average number of times a week students do sport	
Average number of minutes a week students spend doing sport	
Percentage of students who belong to a sports club	
Percentage of students who take part in sports competitions	

5. **Display your results table in the classroom and compare it to other pairs of students. Have you all got the same results? How reliable do you think your results are?**

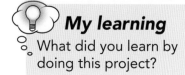

My learning

What did you learn by doing this project?

express opinions, respond to what others say to achieve a shared outcome; draw conclusions

Review 1

Speaking: looking back

Study tip

It's important to look back at what we have studied from time to time. It helps us to remember. So … it's review time!

Look back through Units 1 and 2 and discuss these topics with a partner.

- Find a description of a film you would like to see and explain why you would like to see it.
- Find a picture of a sport that you enjoy doing and explain why you like it.
- Find a picture of a sport that you would like to try and explain why you would like to try it.

Reading: a film review

1 Read and answer the questions.

1 What's the title of the film and who wrote it?

2 What problem do the scientists have?

3 What does the reviewer like and not like about the film?

4 What sort of people does he think will enjoy the film?

2 Would you like to see this film? Why? / Why not?

Into the blue

Into the blue is a new science-fiction film from writer Maya Patel. It tells the story of a group of scientists who travel in a time machine to 2500, but then can't get back again. The special effects are brilliant and the acting is fantastic. The script is slightly disappointing, though.

Recommended for sci-fi fans.

Writing: a fact file

Copy and complete the fact file about your favourite actor or actress.

AN ACTOR / ACTRESS I ADMIRE	
Name	
Date of birth	
Nationality	
First film	
Best film (in your opinion)	
Awards / Prizes	

Vocabulary: films and sports

Can you name:

1 five different types of film?
2 three people who make or are in films?
3 three adjectives you would use to describe films?
4 five different types of sport?
5 three words to describe people involved in sports?
6 three adjectives you would use to describe athletes?

Use of English: future tenses

Choose the correct options to complete the sentences.

> Hi Jane,
>
> Just a quick note to let you know that I ¹_____ my cousins this weekend. My train ²_____ for Vienna at 8.15 tomorrow morning. You're welcome to come too. ³_____ you a ticket? ⁴_____ me know by the end of the day? If you can't come, don't worry! I ⁵_____ send you a postcard.
>
> From,
>
> Sarah

1	a visit	b is going to visit	c am going to visit	d are going to visit
2	a will leaves	b will leave	c leave	d leaves
3	a Shall I get	b I get	c Will you get	d Am I going to get
4	a Shall you let	b Will you let	c Won't you let	d Are you going to let
5	a 'll send	b won't send	c am going to send	d is going to send

Use of English: past tenses

Copy and correct the mistakes in the sentences. One sentence is correct.

1 Last Tuesday, I used to go to the cinema.
2 We were watched the film when the pizza arrived.
3 I was a professional footballer since 2015.
4 While they were running around the park, it started to rain.
5 When I was a little girl, I was playing tennis every week.
6 By the time the race finished, he has already left the stadium.

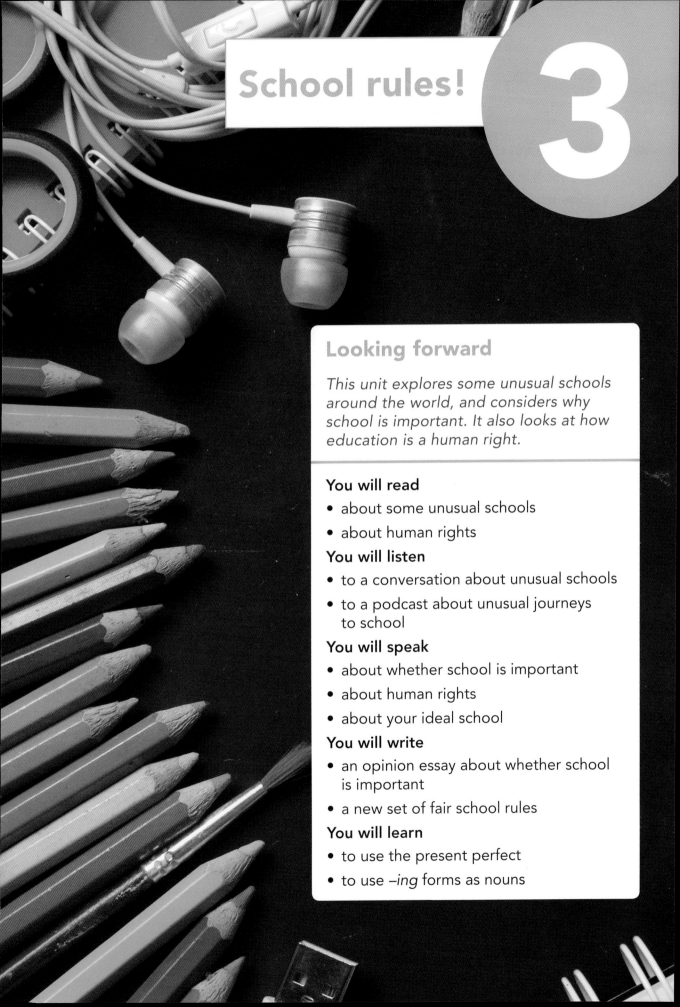

School rules!

3

Looking forward

This unit explores some unusual schools around the world, and considers why school is important. It also looks at how education is a human right.

You will read

- about some unusual schools
- about human rights

You will listen

- to a conversation about unusual schools
- to a podcast about unusual journeys to school

You will speak

- about whether school is important
- about human rights
- about your ideal school

You will write

- an opinion essay about whether school is important
- a new set of fair school rules

You will learn

- to use the present perfect
- to use *–ing* forms as nouns

Travelling schools

1 **Answer the questions.**

- Do you live near your school?
- How do you get to school?
- How long does it take you to get there?

2 **Read the headline and the first paragraph, and look at the pictures. What do you think this article will be about?**

3 **Read the whole article. Were you correct?**

> **Language tip**
> The writer uses the expression: *all aboard*. We say this when we want to tell passengers to get onto a boat, bus or plane.

All aboard for school!

In some parts of the world, people live a very long way from their nearest school. This means that a large number of children miss out on the opportunity of going to school. People have found an answer to this problem – travelling schools!

A number of children in Bangladesh go to school on a boat every day. The first school on a boat opened there in 2002. These boats travel along canals, from village to village, picking up a few children as they go. When the boat is full, the teacher starts the lessons, and at the end of the day, the boat takes the children home again. Energy from the Sun makes electricity for a computer and printer on each boat. Children have three lessons a day, six days a week. It's fun for them, because they enjoy meeting each other on the boat.

Another school that travels to its students is the Solar-Powered Internet School. These schools are inside very large, metal boxes. Lorries, trains or ships can take these boxes to areas without electricity. Each school has a solar-powered whiteboard, and the students use laptops and tablets. A small number of these schools first opened in South Africa in 2011, and since then, more have opened in other countries.

A Solar-Powered Internet School in Africa

The pupils at these schools feel lucky. Kakoli from Bangladesh says, 'I love our school boat. I get excited when it comes. When I grow up, I will be a schoolteacher and teach other children in our village.' Lefa, a student at a Solar-Powered Internet School in South Africa, says, 'I was just happy that finally I would get an opportunity to learn all the things I've always wanted to learn.'

A school boat in Bangladesh

understand main points of a text

4 **What are the main points of the article? Choose the best description.**

a This article is about schools on boats in Bangladesh. A student at the school, Kakoli, talks about her school.

b This article is about special schools in Bangladesh and Africa. These schools bring opportunities to children who don't live near schools.

c This article is about schools in Bangladesh and Africa. Energy from the Sun is useful for these schools. It makes electricity for the whiteboards.

d This article is about the internet in schools in Africa. Some students, for example Lefa, enjoy having the opportunity to learn new things.

5 **Write down the missing numbers or years from these sentences. You have one minute!**

1 The first school boats were used in Bangladesh in
_____.

2 There are _____ lessons a day on the school boat.

3 The school boat works _____ days a week.

4 There is _____ computer on each school boat.

5 The Solar-Powered Internet Schools were first used in
_____.

> **Reading tip**
> When you are looking for a number or a year in a text, you don't have to read every word. Scan your eyes over the words quickly until you see numbers, then read that sentence carefully.

Vocabulary: words in context

1 **Look again at the article. Find five words for things that pupils and teachers can use in a classroom. Do you use these things in your classroom?**

2 **Match the words from the article to the correct definition.**

1	energy	a	powered by energy from the Sun, turning energy into electricity
2	canal	b	situation in which you can do something you want to do
3	solar-powered	c	power
4	opportunity	d	human-made waterway or river

Use of English: reciprocal pronouns.

Read the *Language tip*. Find a reciprocal pronoun in the text on page 30.

Who is meeting on the boat?

> **Language tip**
> *One another* and *each other* are reciprocal pronouns. We use them when two or more people do the same thing. They both have the same meaning but *one another* is a bit more formal.

Listening: talking about unusual schools

1 (3A) **Listen. What are the boys looking at?**

2 Listen again and answer.

1 Why does Leo think the children in the article are unlucky?

2 Why does Sam think they are lucky?

3 Do you think the children who go to travelling schools are lucky or unlucky? Why? Would you like to go to a travelling school? Why? / Why not?

Use of English: present perfect

1 Look at the examples and choose the correct options.

People have found an answer to this problem – travelling schools!

… more have opened in other countries…

These events took place in the ¹[past / present] but are still important in the ²[past / present].

We form the present perfect with *has / have* + ³[*–ing* form / past participle].

2 (3A) **Copy and complete the sentences from the recording. Then listen again to check your answers.**

1 I've _____ finished reading that article about travelling schools.

2 Have you read it _____?

3 I've _____ seen a picture of a school boat before.

4 Have you _____ heard of solar-powered schools?

3 Read and choose the correct options.

1 The words I wrote in Activity 2 are time [adjectives / adverbs].

2 They talk about an indefinite [time up to now / time finished in the past].

3 We often use the [present perfect / past simple] with these words.

4 Ask and answer questions.

1 you / ever / go / on a boat?

2 you / ever / try / surfing?

3 what / you / just / learn?

4 you / finish / this activity / yet?

listen for the main idea and specific information; present perfect

Is school important?

1 **Look and match the different forms of transport.**

1   horse and cart   2   donkey on a mountain path

3   canoe   4   school bus

> **Language tip**
> A *podcast* is a digital audio file that you can download onto your computer, phone or MP3 player and listen to.

a

b

c

d

2 **3B** **Listen and match the countries to the pictures in Activity 1.**

India   China   USA   Indonesia

> **Did you know …?**
> The full name for the country is the *United States of America*. But you will hear people using shortened versions: *the USA, America* or *the States*.

3 **Copy the table. Then listen again and complete it.**

Who?	How do they get to school?	How long does it take?
Patrick from the USA	by [1] _____	[2] _____
Some children in [3] _____	along a mountain [4] _____	five hours
Some children in [5] _____	by canoe	[6] _____
Some children in India	by [7] _____ and cart	[8] _____

4 **Answer the questions.**

1   Why does Patrick do research online about school journeys?

2   Why is the journey the children make in China so dangerous?

3   When can the children in Indonesia not go to school?

4   Why is the journey the children make in India sometimes dangerous?

5 **Do you listen to podcasts in English? Share ideas about good podcasts.**

Use of English: *–ing* form as a noun

1 **3B** **Copy and complete the sentences from Patrick's podcast with the correct form of the verbs in brackets. Then listen again to check your answers.**

1 _____ (get) to school is simple for me.

2 _____ (climb) up a mountain path is the only way children in these areas can get to school.

3 I always enjoy _____ (learn) about people in other countries.

4 _____ (find) out about the lives of these children has taught me a lot.

5 I now understand how important _____ (go) to school is for all of us.

6 Thanks for _____ (listen).

Language tip

When a word ends in *–e*, take off the e before you add *–ing*, for example: *live + ing = writing*.

When a verb with one syllable has consonant – vowel – consonant, double the last letter before adding *–ing*, for example: *sit + ing = sitting*.

2 **Answer these questions.**

1 Are the words in brackets in Activity 1 nouns or verbs?

2 Are the words that you made to complete the sentences in Activity 1 nouns or verbs?

3 How did you change the words?

3 **Copy and complete the text with the correct form of the words from the box.**

listen	hear	travel	learn	choose

¹ _____ to school on a bus can be a bit boring, so I really enjoy ² _____ to podcasts on the journey. I like ³ _____ new things about different people's lives. My favourite podcasts are about music, sports and the news. ⁴ _____ a new podcast to listen to can be confusing because there are so many on the internet. My friends sometimes send me podcasts because they know that I love ⁵ _____ new ones! Maybe one day, I'll make my own!

Speaking: discussion

Read and discuss.

Do you think going to school is important? Why? Why not?

> *Finding out about the lives of these children has taught me a lot because I now understand how important going to school is for all of us.*

Speaking tip

Give reasons for your ideas, using connectives such as *so that, although, while* and *however*.

1 Read the opinions. Who thinks that school is important? Who thinks it isn't important?

> Some people say that you don't need to go to school to get a good education. That's not the way I see it. In my opinion, school is important. We learn how to read and write, and we find out interesting things about the world. For instance, we learn about unusual schools in different countries. **Samira, 13**

> Some people think that school isn't important. I absolutely agree with that idea. As far as I'm concerned, you can learn a lot more by being out in the real world than you can by sitting in a classroom and reading a book about it. For example, look at David Karp, who set up Tumblr in his mother's back bedroom. He left school at 15 and sold Tumblr for $1.1 billion in 2013. **Lisa, 14**

2 Look at the underlined expressions in the texts and find:

1 two ways to talk about what people generally think
2 one way to show you agree with somebody
3 one way to show that you disagree with somebody
4 two ways to introduce your opinion
5 two ways to introduce an example

Writing tip

When you are writing your opinion about something, it is important to develop clear arguments to explain why you feel the way you do. Think of good reasons and examples to support your opinion.

3 What's your opinion? Read the *Writing tip*, then copy and complete the writing plan below.

> ## IS SCHOOL IMPORTANT?
>
> I think that school ... important because ...
>
> Reason 1:
>
> Reason 2:
>
> Example:

4 Write an essay. Use some of the underlined expressions from Activity 2 and your plan from Activity 3.

Read and edit your work. Check your spelling and your grammar.

My learning

Think about your plan and your writing.
Did you complete all the parts of the plan?
Did you follow your plan?
Can you make your plan better?

Focus on Social Studies

Human rights

1 **Read and discuss.**

"A right is not what someone gives you; it's what no one can take from you."
Ramsey Clark

1 What do you think Ramsey Clark means?

2 Can you think of any human rights that we all have?

2 **Match the words to the correct definition.**

1	speech	**a**	anything that belongs to you
2	law	**b**	not in prison
3	property	**c**	a system of rules that a society develops to deal with crime
4	assembly	**d**	only for one person, not for everyone
5	peace	**e**	calm, quiet
6	free	**f**	treating everyone in the same way
7	private	**g**	speaking
8	fair	**h**	a group of people meeting together for a particular purpose

3 **Read the article. Choose the correct words from the box to complete the text in the infographic on the opposite page.**

speech	education	property	assembly	free	private

What are our human rights?

Human rights are the basic rights that we all have because we are human beings. These rights belong to every single person in the world and they cannot be taken away. The United Nations made a list of basic human rights in 1947, to help create peace and make the world a fair place to live. A few of the rights on this list are shown on the infographic on page 37.

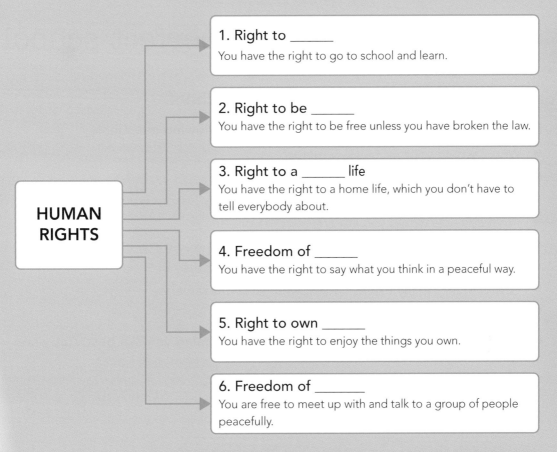

1. Right to _____
You have the right to go to school and learn.

2. Right to be _____
You have the right to be free unless you have broken the law.

3. Right to a _____ life
You have the right to a home life, which you don't have to tell everybody about.

4. Freedom of _____
You have the right to say what you think in a peaceful way.

5. Right to own _____
You have the right to enjoy the things you own.

6. Freedom of _____
You are free to meet up with and talk to a group of people peacefully.

HUMAN RIGHTS

4 **Read the school rules and answer the questions below.**

A Teachers can stop lessons and close the school whenever they want to.

B Teachers can take and keep anything they want from students' bags.

C Students can never give their own opinions and must always agree with the teachers.

D Teachers can lock students in the cupboards whenever they want to.

E Students are not allowed to meet up in groups of two or more in the playground or any part of the school.

F Teachers can ask students' any questions they like about their families and students must answer them.

1 Are these rules fair? Why? / Why not?

2 Match the school rules (A–F) to the basic human rights (1–6) in the infographic above.

5 **Rewrite the school rules in Activity 4 so that they are fair.**

6 **Compare your rules with another student. Who has the fairest rules?**

Project: design your perfect school

Work in a team to design a new, perfect school.

1 **Brainstorm: think of lots of ideas to answer the following questions.**

- Where would your perfect school be?
- How many students and teachers would there be?
- How long would the school day be and how many lessons would there be every day?
- What subjects would you study?
- What would the buildings be like? What activities would you be able to do there?
- Would there be a lot of school rules? What would they be?
- Would there be any exams? If yes, what kind of exams?
- What would your school be called?

2 **Plan: choose which of the ideas from the brainstorming you like best. Copy and complete the school plan.**

| School name: .... SCHOOL | | | |
Location:			
Number of students		School day starts and ends	
Number of teachers		Number of lessons / day	
Subjects studied			
Buildings			
School rules			
Exams taken			

3 **Compare: tell a student from another group about your perfect school. Did you have the same or different ideas?**

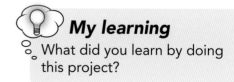

My learning

What did you learn by doing this project?

Bookworms

4

Looking forward

This unit looks at books and reading. You will be able to talk about your favourite books and authors and create your own mini-library.

You will read
- an article about an unusual library
- an extract from a novel

You will listen
- to an interview about why reading is good for us

You will speak
- about books and reading
- about the importance of libraries
- about the advantages and disadvantages of e-readers
- about what books to include in your own Little Free Library

You will write
- about the advantages and disadvantages of e-readers
- a list of books you would like to include in your own Little Free Library

You will learn
- to use questions with prepositions
- to use connectives for contrast

Is reading good for us?

Discuss in groups.

- Are you a bookworm? Why? / Why not?
- What sort of books do you like or not like and why?
- Who is your favourite author?
- What's your favourite book? What was it about and why did you enjoy it so much? Give details and examples.
- Do you think reading is good for you? Why? / Why not?
- Do you think reading can help you to live longer? Why? / Why not?

Listening: an interview with an English professor

1 Read about the *Book Hour* programme and match the words in italics to the correct definition.

2 PM Today's *Book Hour* includes an ¹*interview* with Jane Lay, ²*Professor* of English ³*Literature* at North Hill University. She will be talking about a ⁴*report* which shows that there's a ⁵*connection* between people's reading ⁶*habits* and their health.

a   a senior teacher at a university

b   a relationship between two things

c   books, plays and poetry that people think are high quality

d   a conversation where somebody is asked questions, often for radio or TV

e   things someone does regularly

f   an article that gives information about something

2 What do you think the connection might be between people's reading habits and their health?

3 4A Listen once. What is the connection between people's reading habits and their health? Did you predict correctly in Activity 2?

1 (4A) **Listen again and choose the correct answer.**

1 According to the report, how much longer do readers live compared to non-readers?

   a nearly two months

   b nearly two years

   c more than two years

2 Why do scientists say that reading makes your brain work in a way that helps you to live longer?

   a Reading makes you think deeply and ask questions about what you've read.

   b Reading makes you remember things you've read.

   c Reading is a good way of learning new things.

3 What other reason is given to explain why reading helps people to live a long life?

   a Books help you to ask other people questions.

   b Books help you to understand other people better.

   c Reading books about how the brain works is useful.

4 What two questions does the report *not* answer?

   a Are newspapers better than books? / Does it matter what sort of books you read?

   b Are magazines better than books? / At what age should you start reading?

   c Does it matter what sort of books you read? / At what age should you start reading?

5 Which people took part in this report?

   a 3465 people, aged 15 and over.

   b 3365 people, aged 50 and over.

   c 3635 people, aged 50 and over.

Listening tip

Listen for clues that can help you to understand the detail of a speaker's argument. For example, a speaker might say *Firstly* … and *Secondly* … to introduce more than one point on the same subject.

2 **Discuss.**

- Do you agree that reading can help you to live longer?

- In what other ways do you think reading can be good for you?

Use of English: questions with prepositions

1 (4A) **Look at the pairs of questions. Which questions were used in the interview? Listen again to check your answers.**

a *In which newspaper did this report appear?*

b *Which newspaper did this report appear in?*

a *At what age should you start reading lots of books?*

b *What age should you start reading lots of books at?*

2 **Choose the correct options.**

1 The prepositions come at the [start / end] of the 'a' questions.

2 The prepositions come at the [start / end] of the 'b' questions.

3 The [a / b] questions are used in informal spoken English and the [a / b] questions are used in formal spoken English or written English.

3 **Ask your partner two informal questions with the prepositions at the end and two formal questions with the prepositions at the start.**

Speaking: expressing disbelief and surprise

1 (4B) **Listen again to this section from the interview. Listen to the intonation of the underlined expressions. Which one shows disbelief and which one shows surprise?**

Interviewer: So, tell us, Professor, why is reading books good for our health?

Professor: Well, this report shows that readers live almost two years longer than people who don't read.

Interviewer: Really? I find that hard to believe … In which newspaper did this report appear?

Professor: It appeared in last month's *Social Science and Medicine*.

Interviewer: Oh, OK!

2 **What is the intonation pattern of the underlined words – *fall and then rise* or *rise and then fall*?**

3 **Practise saying the conversation above with your partner.**

4 **Take turns to make similar statements and to respond with the expressions above, using the correct intonation.**

I met Justin Bieber yesterday.

Really?

Well, I met someone who looked a lot like him.

Oh, OK!

Are libraries important?

1 **Discuss.**

- How often do you use your local library or school library? What sorts of books do you borrow?
- In what ways can libraries be important for a local area?
- Do you think every child should have the right to visit a library? Why? / Why not?

2 **Read and think about the headline below. Can you work out what the article will be about?**

3 **Read the article to see if your ideas in Activity 2 were correct.**

Rubbish collector rescues books for Colombian children

Jose Alberto Gutierrez, a **rubbish** collector and book lover from Bogota, Colombia, has collected more than just rubbish over the last 30 years. He has also rescued more than 20 000 books and opened his own library. He says, "Books are the greatest **invention** and the best thing that can happen to a human being."

Gutierrez thinks that books are **luxuries** that poor families cannot **afford** for their children. Although 8.5 million people live in Bogota, there are only 19 public libraries in the city. What is more, these libraries are a long way away from the poor neighbourhoods. Gutierrez thinks that "libraries should be in all neighbourhoods …

this is what Colombia needs." So he decided to make a **community** library, in his own home. Most people's homes are full of furniture, while Gutierrez's house is full of books!

Gutierrez says that it was his mother who gave him his love of reading. She always read to him every night, though she couldn't afford to keep him in school. His favourite authors are Leo Tolstoy, Victor Hugo and Mario Vargas Llosa. A lot of people choose to read **e-books** on **e-readers**, while Gutierrez prefers to read books: "There's nothing more beautiful than having a book in your pocket, in your bag, or inside your car."

4 **Look at the three quotations from Gutierrez in blue in the article. Do you agree or disagree with his opinions? Explain your answers.**

Vocabulary: words in context

Match the correct definition to the words in bold in the article.

1 a digital book you can read on a screen
2 something pleasant and expensive that you want but don't need
3 have enough money to pay for something
4 a group of people who live in an area
5 things you don't want any more
6 a device you can read e-books on
7 something that has been thought of or made for the first time

Reading newspaper articles

1 **Look again at the headline of the article and answer the questions.**

1 Why do newspapers use headlines?
2 Are headlines usually long or short? Why?

2 **Read the *Reading tip* and look again at the first paragraph of the article.**

1 Does it answer the five *Wh–* questions?
2 What are the answers to the *Wh–* questions?

Reading tip
The first paragraph of a newspaper article will often be a summary of the whole story. You may find that it includes all the main points by answering the five *Wh–* questions (*Who? What? Why? When?* and *Where?*) about the story.

Use of English: connectives for contrast

1 **Look again at the article on page 43. Copy and complete these sentences.**

1 _____ 8.5 million people live in Bogota, there are only 19 public libraries in the city.
2 *She always read to him every night, _____ she couldn't afford to keep him in school.*
3 *A lot of people choose to read digital books, _____ Gutierrez prefers to read printed books.*

2 **Read and choose the correct answers.**

1 Connectives are used to [connect / divide] two parts of a sentence, which we call clauses.
2 The connectives *although, though* and *while* are used when the ideas in the clauses are [the same / different].
3 Connectives for contrast [always come at the start of / sometimes come at the start and sometimes in the middle of] the sentence.
4 When we use connectives for contrast, we [use / don't use] commas between the clauses.

analyse the structure of a text; connectives for contrast

Speaking: talking about e-readers

A lot of people choose to read e-books on e-readers, while Gutierrez prefers to read books.

1 **Brainstorm: write down two *advantages* and two *disadvantages* of e-readers compared to books.**

> One advantage of e-readers is that they are easy to carry.

> One disadvantage of e-readers is that the devices are expensive to buy.

2 **Prepare: dealing with words you don't know**

Look again at the speech bubble above right. How would you say that sentence if you didn't know these words?

disadvantage   device   expensive

> One bad thing about e-readers is that ...

Think about how you can use connectives for contrast, such as *although*, *though* and *while*, to link your ideas when you talk.

3 **Discuss: share your ideas about the advantages and disadvantages of e-readers using connectives of contrast to link your ideas. Add your personal opinion.**

Speaking tip

When you're speaking, you may find that you need a word you don't know yet. If this happens, don't stop talking! Use different words to describe the word you don't know. Remember to look up the word you didn't know and write it in your vocabulary book.

> In my opinion, ...

Writing: a discussion essay

What are the advantages and disadvantages of e-readers compared to books?

1 **First, answer the questions to write a plan in your notebook.**

> **PLAN**
>
> **Paragraph 1:** Introduction: What are e-readers?
>
> **Paragraph 2:** What are two advantages of e-readers compared to books?
> *One advantage is ...   Another advantage is ...*
>
> **Paragraph 3:** What are two disadvantages of e-readers compared to books?
> *One disadvantage is ...   A further disadvantage is ...*
>
> **Paragraph 4:** Conclusion: What's your opinion?
> *In my opinion, ...*

Writing tip

Remember to use connectives for contrast, such as *although*, *though* and *while*, to link your ideas when you write.

2 **Write your essay using the useful expressions in the box and connectives for contrast.**

express opinions and justify points of view; develop coherent arguments in writing

Focus on Literature

What makes a good story?

1 **Answer the questions.**

- Do you like reading stories? Why? / Why not?
- Do you like writing stories? Why? / Why not?
- Where do you get your ideas from when you write stories?

2 4B **Read and listen to the start of the book *Wisha Wozzariter* by Payal Kapadia and answer the questions.**

Wisha Wozzariter loved reading. She read before school and after school. She read before lunch and after lunch. She read before dinner and after dinner. She would have read all day and all night if she could.

Wisha hated bad books, but she hated one thing even more: good ones. Good books always left her feeling she could do better if she were to write a book of her own. She'd put down a good book, saying, "Now that's a book I could have written."

On her tenth birthday, Wisha read Roald Dahl's Charlie and the Chocolate Factory. She hated it more than anything. There was no reason something this good should not have been written by her. She got to the last word on the last page, then said, "Now that's a book I could have written!"

"Why don't you?" said a green little worm, popping his head out of page number 64.

"Who are you?" asked Wisha, startled.

"Why, a Bookworm, who else?" said the worm, sounding surprised. "I've heard you

say the same thing after every good book. So why don't you?"

"Why don't I – what?" said Wisha.

"Write a book, write a book," said the Bookworm in a sing-song voice.

"I wish I was a writer," said Wisha.

"Well, you are Wisha Wozzariter," said the Bookworm.

"So I am! But I don't quite know where to begin."

"At the beginning, of course," said the Bookworm. "Got some time?"

"Yee-es. Why, what do you suggest?" asked Wisha.

"A trip to the Marketplace of Ideas," said the Bookworm.

Wisha jumped up, "Sounds more exciting than wishing all day! How do we get there?"

"Close your eyes and hold my hand tight," said the Bookworm. "We're catching the Thought Express."

1 What book does Wisha wish she had written?
2 Where does the Bookworm come from?
3 What does the Bookworm tell Wisha to do?
4 Why is Wisha Wozzariter's *name* important?
5 Where are Wisha and the Bookworm going to go and how are they going to travel there?

3 **Read and discuss.**

> The Bookworm takes Wisha on an exciting adventure looking for the important parts of a story. On the way, she finds her Imagination, an Idea, a Hero, her own Style, a Structure (a Beginning, a Middle and an End).

- Do you agree that these are the most important things for a story to have? Why / Why not?
- Would you add anything else?

4 **Read the end of the story. What is the last thing the Bookworm tells Wisha every story should have? Do you agree? Where is the Bookworm at the end of the story?**

"Is this lunch?" said Wisha.

"Go on, bite into it," said the Bookworm. "It's a Truth Sandwich."

"I'm very hungry," said Wisha, laughing. "It will take a lot more than this to fill me up."

"Eat it," said the Bookworm. "You'll be surprised how good the Truth can be."

"How does it taste?" asked Wisha, smelling the sandwich.

"It's a little bitter," said the Bookworm. "But it wouldn't be the Truth if it wasn't."

Wisha bit into the sandwich. It didn't taste good or bad. It tasted like what it was. The Truth. Plain and simple.

That's how it is with things. They always work out in The End …

So Wisha wrote her story. This story. The story of how she became a writer. A story about Wisha's adventures on the Thought Express and all the strange places it took her to. A story about how Wisha learnt to use her Imagination ... But in The End, a story about how Wisha stopped wishing and started writing.

And what of the Bookworm? The last time Wisha saw him, he was in her book. On page 77. And he looked pleased.

5 **Discuss.**
- What words would you use to describe the characters Wisha and the Bookworm? Do you like them? Why? / Why not?
- Payal Kapadia describes ideas as things, for example: the *Marketplace of Ideas*, the *Thought Express*, a *Truth Sandwich*. Do you like this way of describing things? Do you think it makes the story easier to understand? Why? / Why not?
- Would you recommend this story to a friend? Why? / Why not?

Project: make a Little Free Library

1 Read about the Little Free Library project and answer the questions.

Little Free Library

In 2009, Todd Bol from the USA built the first Little Free Library. It's a small box, which he filled with books and put outside his house for people to borrow. There are now more than 50 000 Little Free Libraries all over the world. These help people to read more and create a strong sense of community, as well.

- Do you think the Little Free Library is a good idea? Why? / Why not?
- Why do you think these help to create a strong sense of community?

2 You are going to work in groups to make a Little Free Library. Discuss what types of books you would like to include. Think of any other types of books you would like.

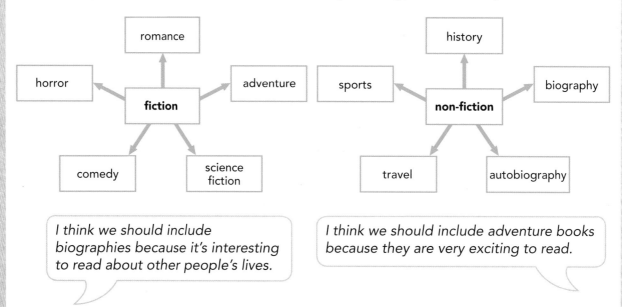

I think we should include biographies because it's interesting to read about other people's lives.

I think we should include adventure books because they are very exciting to read.

3 Choose three books each to include. Write a list of the titles and authors that your group has chosen. Swap your list with another group. Did you choose any of the same books?

4 Make a Little Free Library in one corner of your classroom. Bring in a book to share, and borrow and read a new book.

My learning
What did you learn by doing this project?

Review 2

Speaking: the main points of a news story

Discuss in pairs.

1 Look again at these photos What were the main points in the stories they illustrated? Can you remember three or more for each story?

2 Read the texts on pages 30 and 43 quickly. Did you remember correctly? What did you forget?

3 Which of these stories did you find the most interesting and why?

Listening: what's missing?

1 **This is part of the podcast you heard in Unit 3. Write down the correct words to complete the paragraph.**

There are some villages high up in the mountains in ¹_____ Climbing up a mountain path is the only way children in these areas can get to school. Some children go by ²_____ The journey is dangerous and long. In some places, the path is only 40 cm wide and it takes them five hours to get to school. It is the only school in the area and there's only one teacher.

Children in other countries have dangerous journeys too. In some areas of ³_____ , children go to school by ⁴_____ . They travel from their villages for an hour to get to their schools. When the weather is bad, they cannot go to school at all. In ⁵_____ , children sometimes go to school on the back of a ⁶_____ . Some children travel for two hours and often a lot of children travel in the same cart, which it is very dangerous.

2 **3A** **Now listen and check your answers. How many did you get right?**

Writing: your opinion

1. You're going to write an opinion essay: *Are libraries important?* Copy and complete the plan.

> I think that libraries (are / aren't) important because …
>
> Reason 1:
>
> Reason 2:
>
> Example:

2. Write your essay. Use some of the useful expressions from page 35.

3. Read and edit your essay. Check:
   - Have I thought of good reasons?
   - Have I used any useful expressions?
   - Have I spelled all the words correctly and used the correct punctuation?

4. Swap with a partner and compare your ideas.

Vocabulary: talking about books

1. Think of as many different types of fiction as you can. Which do you like best and why?

2. Think of as many different types of non-fiction as you can. Which do you like best and why?

Use of English: present perfect

1. Make questions.
   1. you / ever / read / an autobiography?
   2. you / ever / read / a horror story?
   3. what book / you / just / finish?
   4. you / learn / how to use / present perfect / yet?

2. Ask and answer the questions in pairs.

Use of English: connectives for contrast

Copy and complete the sentences with your own ideas.
1. I like reading books, though …
2. Alex loves watching dramas, while …
3. My brother goes to the cinema every week, while …
4. Although I like films, …

Extreme weather

Looking forward

This unit explores extreme weather, and considers in detail the causes and effects of flooding.

You will read
- a blog post about an extreme weather event
- some text messages about extreme weather
- an extract from a geography textbook about flooding

You will listen
- to some weather forecasts

You will speak
- about extreme weather
- about the causes and effects of flooding

You will write
- a descriptive blog post about an extreme weather event

You will learn
- to use present simple and past simple passive
- to use adjectives with *–ing* and *–ed* endings
- to use demonstrative pronouns

What is extreme weather?

Vocabulary: extreme weather

Match the pictures to the words and phrases.

| thick fog | a cold spell | a drought | heavy rainfall and floods | a hurricane | a heat wave |

a

b

c

d

e

f

Speaking: talking about extreme weather

Discuss.

1 What problems can extreme weather cause?

2 Have you ever experienced extreme weather? What was it like and what did you do?

3 Where can we find weather forecasts?

4 What is a severe weather warning?

5 What sort of advice might you hear in a severe weather warning?

Listening: weather forecasts

1 (5) **Listen and match the weather forecasts (1–6) with the photographs above (a–f).**

2 (5) **Listen again and answer the questions.**

1 Forecast 1: When is the hurricane going to end?

2 Forecast 2: How much snow is expected to fall in the south-west?

3 Forecast 3: Who is advised to take extra care in hot conditions?

4 Forecast 4: In what part of the country is fog expected tomorrow?

5 Forecast 5: When is rain expected in the east of the country?

6 Forecast 6: How much rain is expected to fall?

Use of English: present simple passive and past simple passive

1 🔊 **Listen again. Copy and complete the sentences.**

1 *A severe weather warning _____ today.*
2 *People _____ to expect up to 15 cm of snow.*
3 *Elderly people _____ **by** health experts yesterday to take extra care.*
4 *Thick fog _____ in many south-eastern parts of the country.*

2 **Look at the sentences in Activity 1. Copy and complete the grammar rules with words from the box.**

am / is / are + past participle	*was / were* + past participle
by past simple passive	present simple passive

1 Sentences 2 and 4 are in the _____ .
2 Sentences 1 and 3 are in the _____ .
3 The present simple passive is formed with _____ .
4 The past simple passive is formed with _____ .
5 We don't usually say who did the action of the verb in the passive, but if we do, then we use the word _____ .

3 **Copy and complete with the words *active* or *passive*.**

We use a(n) ¹ _____ verb when we want to focus on the person or thing doing the action. We use a(n) ² _____ verb when we want to focus on the person or thing who receives the action. So we often hear the ³ _____ in reports, such as weather forecasts, when we don't know or aren't interested in who did the action of the verb.

> ### Listening tip
> In weather reports, you will often hear compass points to describe places and words to describe weather conditions or talk about temperature. Also, you will hear the future tense with *will* and *going to* for predictions. With severe weather warnings, you may hear phrases giving advice, too.

Listening: features of weather forecasts

5 🔊 **Read the *Listening tip*, then listen again. Work in pairs, Student A and Student B.**

Student A, make notes of:	**Student B**, make notes of:
• two compass directions	• two different temperatures
• two descriptions of weather conditions	• two pieces of advice
• two examples of future tenses	• two examples of future tenses

> In Forecast 1, I heard the weather forecaster say north.

> In Forecast 2, I heard −10 degrees Celsius.

Talking about extreme weather

1 **Read Bruno's blog post. Which photograph goes with the blog post?**

a
b
c

MY BLOG

Tuesday, 14 March

A TERRIFYING NIGHT

It was just before midnight and I woke up suddenly. I sat up in bed, terrified and shocked. I was alone in the house, so what was that noise? I realised that my bedroom window was shaking loudly. That is what had woken me up. I went to the
5   window and opened it to look at the storm. It was amazing and terrifying at the same time!

I saw some flashes of lightning far away, which were lighting up the night sky. Those looked like long, thin, bright arms reaching down to the ground. The rain was falling heavily,
10 then suddenly I heard the shocking noise of thunder. That sounded as loud as a drum beating in my ears. I could also hear the cries of wolves, but I tried to ignore those.

The rain that fell on my face and arms was as cold as ice. The raindrops that ran down my neck felt like little, frozen,
15 icy rivers. These made me feel very cold in my thin pyjamas. I could smell the fresh grass as the rain fell on it. The storm was clearing and the sun was coming up. I felt like I could actually taste the new day.

Then the storm was over, and I felt disappointed and then
20 suddenly quite exhausted. Everyone else in the house was still asleep, which was disappointing. I closed the bathroom window and quietly went back to bed. What a night!

Bruno Rossi

Language tip

A *blog* is a website that describes the daily life of the person who writes it, and also their thoughts and ideas. A blog is usually written in the first person and the person who writes a blog is called a *blogger*.

Punctuation tip

Note how we use commas between adjectives in a list:

long, thin, bright arms

little, frozen, icy rivers

2 Read the *Reading tip*, then find three things in the blog post on page 54 that don't make sense.

Use of English: adjectives with *–ing* and *–ed* endings

1 In the blog post on page 54, find five adjectives ending in *–ing* and five adjectives ending in *–ed*.

2 Look at the examples you found and answer the questions.

1 Which adjective ending is used to describe how somebody feels?

2 Which adjective ending is used to describe the cause of a feeling?

3 Use some of the *–ed* adjectives that you found in Activity 1 to describe how you feel today. Explain why you feel this way using some of the *–ing* adjectives.

Use of English: pronouns for textual reference

1 Read the *Language tip*, then find one example of each pronoun (*this, that, these* and *those*) in the blog post on page 54. What do the pronouns refer to in each sentence?

> *I realised that my bedroom window was shaking loudly. This is what had woken me up.*
>
> The pronoun *this* in line 4 refers to the noise the window was making.

Reading tip

Sometimes, you may find that a writer says one thing in a text, then later says something else that is different from what they said before. Don't worry if you find things in a text that don't seem to make sense. This just means you are becoming a better reader!

Language tip

The pronouns *this, that, these* and *those* are often used to point to something, for example:

***That's** my hat.*

They are also used instead of nouns to refer to something that has recently been mentioned in a sentence, for example:

*He lost his hat. **That's** why he's cold.*

2 Think of your own sentences using *this, that, these* and *those* to refer to something that has already been mentioned.

Speaking: talking about blogs

Discuss.

- Do you think that Bruno describes the storm well in his blog post? Why / Why not?
- Do you like reading blogs? Why / Why not?
- Share ideas for different blogs that you can read.

---

recognise inconsistencies in reading; participle adjectives; demonstrative pronouns   55

Writing: descriptions

1 Read the *Writing tip* and find examples of descriptions using the five senses in the blog post on page 54. Do you think these are good descriptions? Why? / Why not?

2 Copy and complete the similes from the text and discuss the questions.

> a The lightning looked _____ long arms reaching down to the ground.
>
> b The thunder sounded _____ loud _____ a terrifying drum.
>
> c The rain that fell on my face and arms was _____ cold _____ ice.
>
> d The raindrops that ran down my neck felt _____ little icy rivers.

1 What two things are being compared in each of the similes above?

2 Why do you think this is a good way of describing something?

Writing tip

A good way to make your descriptive writing more interesting is to use your five different senses (sight, hearing, smell, touch and taste).

You can also use *similes*, which is a way of comparing two things using *like* or *as*:

*The rain sounded **like** drums on the roof. It was **as** loud **as** a brass band.*

Writing: a descriptive blog post

Choose one of the photographs below and imagine that you are the person in the picture. Write a blog post about what the weather is like.

Read your work and ask yourself the following questions:

- Have I written interesting descriptions using some or all of the senses?
- Have I used similes?
- Have I used commas in between adjectives in lists ? (see *Punctuation tip* on page 54)

identify descriptive features in texts; write a descriptive text

Texting about the weather

Reading: text messages

Reading tip

Sometimes a writer does not say exactly what they mean. So, think about *how* a writer says things, not just what they say. Consider what situation the writer is in and how they feel about it. Are they happy or sad? Are they being funny or serious?

1 Read the *Reading tip*. Then read the text messages and choose the correct options.

Milk finished! Cold and windy out! Lots homework. Mum, you pass the shop, don't u?!

1 What is Sam asking his mother to do?
   a make him some breakfast
   b help him with his homework
   c buy some milk on her way home

VVVV cold today. No gloves! Wish I had some. Glad it's my bday soon! C u 2mrw @ my party!!

2 What's Sarah really saying in this message?
   a It's cold in the mornings.
   b She's going to buy some gloves.
   c She wants some gloves for her birthday.

HEAVY rain, no umbrella, not seen since you borrowed it Leo???? Dad

3 What does Dad think happened to his umbrella?
   a He thinks that he lost it last time he used it.
   b He thinks his son, Leo, has it or has lost it.
   c He thinks it's in the cupboard somewhere.

2 Discuss.
   1 How many text messages do you write every week?
   2 Why do you usually write text messages?
   3 How are text messages different from other forms of written English?

Focus on Geography

Floods

1 **Read and match the words with the correct definition.**

1	urbanisation	a	what makes an event happen
2	deforestation	b	a reaction to something
3	refugee camp	c	the result of something
4	response	d	some time in the future
5	cause	e	the cutting down of the trees in an area
6	effect	f	the turning of countryside into towns or cities
7	immediate	g	now or very soon
8	long-term	h	a place to stay for people who have had to leave their homes for safety reasons

2 **Discuss.**

1 Have you ever been in a flood?

2 What do you think are the main problems facing people whose homes are flooded?

3 Do you know what causes floods?

4 Do you know about any bad floods that have happened in the world?

    a What were the causes of these floods?

    b What effects did they have?

    c How did people respond to them?

3 **Read the explanation about why rivers flood. Then look at the case study on the next page. Choose the correct words from the box to fill the gaps.**

> immediate   causes   long-term   effects

Language tip

A case study is an example of a particular type of event, for example, the Mozambique floods is a case study for the topic of flooding. You will often need to use a case study in Geography to explain a general point, for example, you could talk about the causes of the Mozambique flood as a way of talking about the causes of floods in general.

Why do rivers flood?

A river floods when the water gets high enough to run into the area around it. Rivers flood because of:

- heavy rainfall over a short period of time or long periods of rain

- hurricanes, cyclones or typhoons

- urbanisation, because towns and cities have more buildings and roads that the water can't get through

- deforestation, because trees can slow or stop flood water.

CASE STUDY: Mozambique floods, 2000

What were the [1] _____ **of the floods?**

- Heavy rainfall in southern Africa for almost five weeks: there is usually 177 mm of rainfall in February, but there was 1163 mm that year.

- Cyclone Eline hit the area on 22 February, which made things worse.

What were the [2] _____ **of the floods?**

- About 800 people died.

- 250 000 people lost their homes.

- 140 000 hectares of farmland were lost and 113 000 small farms lost everything.

- Many schools were closed, so 214 000 children had no classroom.

What was the [3] _____ **response?**

- Mozambican boats rescued over 45 000 people from rooftops and trees.

- Refugee camps were set up.

What was the [4] _____ **response?**

- Rescue equipment came from Europe and North America three weeks after the flood.

- Mozambican government asked for $450 million from the international community for new roads, health units and schools.

Mozambique

4 Read again. Copy and complete the sentences with a word or number.

1 A flood can be caused by a long period of _____.

2 There was very bad flooding in Mozambique in the year _____.

3 _____ people waited on roofs and trees for rescue.

4 _____ children were left without a school.

5 The government in Mozambique asked the rest of the world for $_____ to help them.

5 Look again at questions 3 and 4 in Activity 2 and answer them without looking at the text.

6 Discuss.

1 Look again at the section *Why do rivers flood*? Which two are human-made causes rather than natural causes? How can we avoid these things?

2 Look again at the responses to the Mozambique floods. Do you think that the responses were good enough or quick enough? What else could people have done to help?

3 Discuss how and why these methods for reducing flooding might work:

   a make rivers straighter, deeper and wider   b plant more trees.

Project: a case study of an extreme weather event

1 You are going to work in groups to write a case study and give a presentation about an extreme weather event. Decide what sort of extreme weather you would like to focus on, for example, flooding, hurricanes or droughts.

Project tip

Remember that you are going to use this case study to make general points about this type of weather event, so choose a good example where there is a lot to talk about.

2 Read the *Project tip*, then choose a particular example of this type of extreme weather event, for example, the Mozambique floods of 2000.

3 Research these questions. Assign different questions to different members of the group.

- What's the name of the weather event you have chosen?

- Where did it happen?

- When did it happen?

- What were the causes?

- What were the effects?

- What were the immediate responses?

- What were the long-term responses?

4 Write your case study together.

- Use a large piece of paper, so it can be shown to the class.

- Use the same layout as the case study on page 59 or design your own. Remember to make it as easy to understand as possible.

- Use photographs or maps to illustrate what you are saying.

5 Read and edit your work. Check your spelling and your grammar.

My learning

What did you learn by doing this project?

6 Prepare and give a presentation about your case study. Take turns to talk about the different sections.

7 Look at the other case studies and listen to the presentations. Ask questions.

interact to achieve a shared outcome; link ideas into a coherent extended talk

Extreme planet

6

Looking forward

This unit looks at some of the most extreme environments and animals on our planet, and gives you the opportunity to design your own world tour.

You will read

- an article about extreme places on Earth
- an article about an extreme world tour

You will listen

- to a presentation about important animals

You will speak

- about where you've been on our planet
- about the most important species
- about where you would like to go on a world tour

You will write

- an opinion essay about the most important species
- about travel plans

You will learn

- to use non-defining relative clauses
- to use the present continuous passive

Extreme places

Speaking: talking about our planet

1 **Discuss.**

- What's the highest place you've ever been to?
- What's the biggest natural thing you've ever seen?
- What are the hottest / coldest temperatures you've ever felt?
- What's the most interesting place in the world you've ever been to? Why was it so amazing?

2 **Look and match the photographs with the places. Which place would you most like to visit and why?**

Amazon river and rainforest

Pacific Ocean islands and rocks

peak of Mount Everest

3 **Do a quiz to find out how much you know about our planet. If you don't know the answer, guess!**

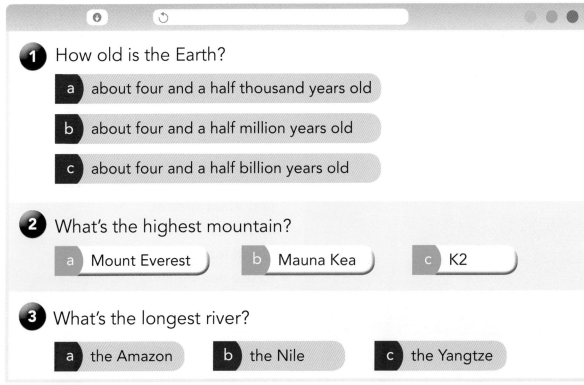

1 How old is the Earth?

- a about four and a half thousand years old
- b about four and a half million years old
- c about four and a half billion years old

2 What's the highest mountain?

- a Mount Everest
- b Mauna Kea
- c K2

3 What's the longest river?

- a the Amazon
- b the Nile
- c the Yangtze

describe experiences; express opinions

1 Read the article quickly and choose the best title. You have one minute!

MARVELLOUS PEOPLE ON OUR PLANET

Marvellous planets in space

OUR MARVELLOUS PLANET

> **Language tip**
> When we don't know or don't want to say an exact number we can use:
>
> *approximately 4.54 billion years old*
> *about 6670 kilometres long*
> *around 6400 kilometres long*

2 Read again and complete the article with the correct form of the words in the box.

> the hottest place   the largest ocean   the longest river
> the highest mountain   the coldest place   the biggest forest

The Earth is incredible.

Scientists, who have looked carefully at many different types of rock on our planet, think that it's approximately 4.54 billion years old.

Many people think that Mount Everest in Nepal, Asia, is [1]_____ in the world. It's 8848 metres above sea level. However, there's another one that is 10 210 metres from the bottom to the top. This is a huge volcano in Hawaii, Mauna Kea. Interestingly, though, only 4205 metres of it is above sea level, and the rest – more than half of it – is below sea level. Mount Everest, however, remains the
10 ultimate challenge for mountaineers. Edmund Hilary, who came from New Zealand, was the first person to climb to the top of Mount Everest with Tenzing Norgay in 1953.

[2]_____ is the Nile in Egypt, Africa, which is about 6650 kilometres long. Another river that is very long is the Amazon River in South America. This runs through several countries and is around 6400 kilometres long.

[3]_____ in the world is the gigantic Amazon rainforest, where more than one-third of all species of animals live. The rainforest is also home to millions of people, who use the forest for shelter and food.
20 It's 6.5 million square kilometres, which is almost as enormous as Australia.

[4]_____ is the magnificent Pacific Ocean, which is 155 million square kilometres.
25 There's enough space in this ocean to fit all the world's continents!

[5]_____ on Earth is Al Aziziyah in Libya, where it reached 57.8°C on 13 September 1922.

[6]_____ is in Russia at the Vostok Station,
30 where the temperature never goes above zero. This Antarctic station, whose winter population is only 13 scientists and engineers, reached a temperature low of –89.2°C on 21 July 1983.

3 Check your answers to the questions in Activity 3, *Speaking: talking about our planet.*

4 Which of these places would you most and least like to visit and why?

Reading: finding specific information

Look again at the article on page 63. Answer the questions.

1 How old is our planet?
2 How high is Mauna Kea from the bottom to the top?
3 Which river is 6400 kilometres long?
4 In what part of the world can we find one-third of all animal species?
5 What temperature was reached in Al Aziziyah on 13 September 1922?
6 What temperature was reached in the Antarctic on 21 July 1983?

Vocabulary: extreme adjectives

Put the adjectives from the text in the correct word set.

huge   incredible   marvellous   gigantic
magnificent   enormous

extremely good

extremely big

Language tip

Note how we talk about size and temperature. We use:

metres to say how high or long something is: *Mauna Kea is 10 210 **metres high**. / The Nile is 6650 **kilometres long**.*

square kilometres to say the area of something: *The Amazon rainforest is 6.5 **million square kilometres**.*

degrees Celsius to talk about temperature: *A temperature low of **−89°C**.*

Vocabulary: words in context

Match the words from the article with the correct definition.

1 rock
2 ocean
3 volcano

4 continent
5 population
6 rainforest
7 species
8 peak

a a very large area of land, for example, Asia or Africa
b a thick forest of tall trees in a wet area
c one of the five very large areas of salty water on Earth, for example, the Pacific or Atlantic
d a related group of plants or animals
e hard material in the ground and mountains
f a mountain that throws out hot liquid, rock and fire
g the top of a mountain
h all the people who live in a country or area

1 Copy and complete the sentences from the article on page 63 with
which, where or *who*.

1 *Scientists, _____ have looked carefully at many different types of rock on the planet, think that it's approximately 4.54 billion years old.*

2 *Most people think that the highest mountain in the world is Mount Everest in Nepal, _____ is 8848 metres above the sea.*

3 *The biggest forest in the world is the gigantic Amazon rainforest, _____ more than one-third of all species of animals live.*

2 Find two other examples of relative clauses with each relative pronoun in the article.

3 Copy and complete the grammar rules with the words from the box.

which	who	where	commas

1 We use _____ around non-defining relative clauses.
2 We use _____ to talk about people.
3 We use _____ to talk about things.
4 We use _____ to talk about places.

4 Make one sentence instead of two using a relative clause.

1 The deepest place on Earth is the Mariana Trench. The Mariana Trench is 10916 metres below the sea.

2 Roald Amundsen was the first man to get to the South Pole. Roald Amundsen came from Norway.

3 The wettest place in the world is Mawsynram. Mawsynram is in India.

4 The world's highest city is Peru's La Rinconada. About 50000 people live in La Rinconada.

5 Make three new sentences of your own using *which, who* or *where* to add information.

> ### Punctuation tip
>
> Non-defining clauses can come in the middle of a sentence with a comma before and after.
>
> *Edmund Hillary, who came from New Zealand, was the first person to climb to the top of Mount Everest.*
>
> They can also come at the end of the sentence with a comma before and a full stop after:
>
> *The longest river in the world is the Nile, which is about 6650 kilometres long.*

Mawsynram in India is the wettest place in the world.

Extreme animals

Listening: important animals

1 Match the words with the correct definition.

1	hunt	a	go away
2	disappear	b	environment in which an animal or plant lives and grows
3	destroy	c	chase and kill wild animals for food
4	recycle	d	cause so much damage that something can't be used again
5	habitat	e	an illness
6	disease	f	change something so it can be used again

2 Match the words in the box to the photos in Activity 3.

bee   humans   mushrooms   apes   snake   mosquito

3 🔊 Listen and choose the correct options.

1 Which species does Natasha think is the most dangerous in the world?

a    b    c

2 Which species does she think is the most important in the world?

a    b    c

4 🔊 Read the *Listening tip*. Natasha uses questions and answers in her presentation. Listen again and write down the questions for these answers.

1 Many people will say humans.

2 It's because they're our closest relatives.

3 As far as I'm concerned, it's bees.

> **Listening tip**
> We sometimes ask and answer questions when we talk, particularly in presentations. You need to understand the questions so that you can understand the answers.

5 Use your own ideas to answer these questions about what Natasha said.

1 Why do you think scientists disagree about the most dangerous and most important species?

2 Why do you think that humans could be the most dangerous species?

3 Why is the fact that apes are our closest relatives important?

4 Why do you think apes are important for tourism in parts of Africa?

listen for the main points and specific information; express opinions

Use of English: present continuous passive

1 **6))** **Listen again, copy and complete the phrases from the recording.**

1 *Hundreds of thousands of people _____ every year.*
2 *This important insect _____ in danger by disease and climate change.*
3 *Their habitat _____ and they _____ for their meat.*

2 **Look at the examples and answer the questions.**

1 When we want to focus on a person or thing who is doing an action, do we use the active or passive?
2 When we want to focus on a person or thing who is receiving an action, do we use the active or passive?
3 How do we form the present continuous passive?

3 **Write these sentences in the passive.**

1 People are destroying this natural environment.
2 People are cutting down forests to make way for roads.
3 People are measuring rainfall all over the world.

> ## Speaking tip
>
> Everyone's opinion is important. Don't be shy to give your point of view about a topic. Explain and justify how you feel by giving good reasons or examples. Make sure you listen to other people's opinions, too!

Speaking: giving your opinion

1 **Read the *Speaking tip*, then put the phrases in the correct group.**

In my opinion, …   *I feel this way because …*
This is my opinion because …   *As far as I'm concerned, …*

(to introduce your opinion)   (to explain your opinion)

2 **Discuss. Use the phrases from Activity 1 to introduce and explain your opinions.**

- What do you think is the most dangerous species and why?
- What do you think is the most important species and why?

Writing: your opinion

Write an opinion essay: What do you think is the most important species and why?

Read your work and ask yourself the following questions:

- Have I included my ideas from Speaking: giving your opinion?
- Have I included useful phrases for introducing and explaining my point of view from Speaking: giving your opinion?
- Have I given reasons and examples to justify my opinion?
- Have I used non-defining relative clauses with the correct punctuation?
- Have I used some of the vocabulary that I have learned in this unit?

Focus on the World

Extreme tour of the world

1 Match the words with the correct definition.

1	destination	**a**	a solid shape with a flat base and four sides that form a point at the top where they meet
2	rollercoaster	**b**	a celebration in the street with music and dancing
3	pyramid	**c**	a piece of art that is made into a shape from a material like stone or wood
4	sculpture	**d**	a place where water flows over a steep part of a hill and falls into a pool below
5	carnival	**e**	an extreme ride at an amusement park
6	waterfall	**f**	the place you are going to

2 Read and match the continents below to the parts of the texts.

> Asia   Africa   Europe   North America   South America   Oceania

Would you like to visit the most unusual and the most exciting destinations in all six continents of the world? Then, fasten your seatbelts and read on!

1 _____

Visit Valencia in Spain to take part in the world's biggest food fight! Every August, tens of thousands of people throw 150 tonnes of tomatoes at each other!

Go to the world's largest ice building, the ice hotel in Sweden. The hotel doesn't last all year, so it is built again every autumn out of 35 000 cubic metres of snow and ice, which is the same as 700 million snowballs!

2 _____

Have a ride on the steepest rollercoaster in the world in Fujiyoshida City, Japan. The ride only lasts 112 seconds, but you won't forget it that quickly!

Visit the longest wall in the world, the Great Wall of China. Built over 2000 years ago, the main wall is 3460 kilometres long, and you can walk along parts of it and enjoy magnificent views.

read extended non-fiction text

3 _____

Explore the world's tallest pyramid, the Great Pyramid at Giza, Egypt. It was built about 4500 years ago, and is an enormous 137.5 metres tall.

Visit the world's biggest mud building, the Great Mosque in Djenné, Mali. Its marvellous red walls sometimes get damaged in heavy rainfall, so the building is repaired with fresh mud every year.

4 _____

Visit the biggest banana, the biggest pineapple or the biggest penguin in the world! Australia's Big Things are unusual, large sculptures that are placed all around the country.

Stand on top of the largest rock in the world, which is also in Australia – Uluru is an incredible 348 metres high and 2.5 kilometres long!

5 _____

Visit the world's oldest national park – Yellowstone National Park in the USA. It has been a national park since 1872 and is a great place to enjoy nature. You can even camp there!

Stand on top of the world's most visited waterfalls – the Niagara Falls on the border between Canada and the USA. Twenty-two and a half million people visit every year, so you won't be alone!

6 _____

Swim in the largest swimming pool in Chile. It's 1013 metres long, with an area of eight hectares. You can even sail a boat on it!

Enjoy the largest carnival in the world at Rio de Janeiro in Brazil. It is held over four days in February or March, and about two million people visit every day.

3 **Read again and choose the best destination for these people.**

1 Rita: I enjoy learning about history and I love going for long walks.

2 Tom: I'm really interested in unusual art, the stranger the better!

3 Zoe: I like dancing and I think street parties are such fun!

4 Carlos: I like scary rides at amusement parks! There's nothing too scary for me!

5 Laurence: I'm really interested in learning about ancient civilizations, like the Romans, Greeks or Egyptians.

6 Jamie: I love camping because it makes me feel really close to nature.

4 **Which of the destinations would you most like to visit and why?**

Project: plan a world tour

You are going to work in groups to make a poster and give a presentation about a world tour.

1 Choose your destinations. Discuss and decide on one place to visit on each continent. You can use some of the ideas from this unit or find your own ideas.

Asia	Africa
Europe	North America
South America	Oceania

2 Plan your journey. Where are you going to start and in what order are you going to travel around the world? How long are the journeys going to take?

3 Make a poster to show your plans. Include:

- where you're going and what you're going to do in each place
- your travel plans
- a map and photographs.

4 Review your poster.

- Have you remembered to include all the information you need?
- Have you spelled the place names correctly?

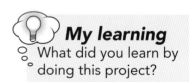

My learning
What did you learn by doing this project?

5 Prepare and give a presentation about your tour. Take turns to talk about the different continents and explain your choice of destinations.

6 Look at the other posters, listen to the presentations and ask questions. Who is planning to visit the most unusual place?

interact to achieve a shared outcome; link ideas into a coherent extended talk

Review 3

Speaking: looking back

Look back through Units 5 and 6. Discuss.

- Which activity did you enjoy the most? Say why you liked it and what you learned from doing it.
- What was the most interesting fact that you learned? Explain why you found this interesting.

Reading: a quiz

1 **Work in pairs. Find the answers to these questions in Units 5 and 6.**

   1 What are the two scales that are used to talk about temperature?

   2 What is a blog?

   3 What is a simile?

   4 How old is the Earth?

   5 What's the longest river in the world and how long is it?

   6 What's the biggest forest in the world and how big is it?

2 **Write six more questions to ask about Units 5 and 6.**

3 **Work with another pair. Ask and answer their questions.**

Listening: a weather forecast

1 **Complete the weather forecast that you heard in Unit 5 with the words from the box.**

> hurricane   night   10 a.m.   severe   Saturday   120 kilometres   north   winds

> There's a ¹___ weather warning for the ²___ of the country from ³___ on ⁴___ . Hurricane Henry will bring extremely powerful ⁵___ of up to ⁶___ per hour. People are advised to plan ahead and be prepared. The ⁷___ is expected to move away by Sunday ⁸___ .

2 🔊 **Listen again and check your answers.**

Writing: a description

1 **Imagine that you are the person in the photograph on the right. Write a description of what the weather is like.**

   Remember to include:

   - interesting descriptions using some or all of your senses
   - similes.

2 **Swap descriptions with a partner. Tell your partner what you like best about their description.**

Vocabulary: extreme weather and planet

Discuss.

- Name three types of extreme weather. Have you ever experienced these types of weather?
- Name three adjectives that end with –*ed* and three adjectives that end with –*ing*.
- What's the difference between an –*ed* and an –*ing* adjective?
- Name six natural features of our planet (for example, *a forest*). Which of these features have you seen?
- Name two adjectives that mean *extremely good* and two adjectives that mean *extremely big*. Use them in sentences.

Use of English: the passive form and adding information

1 **Work in pairs, Student A and Student B. Complete the tasks in your box.**

> **Student A**
>
> **Write these sentences in the passive.**
>
> 1 The hurricane destroyed the house.
> 2 People are hunting crocodiles in this area.
> 3 Someone cut down that tree last week.
>
> **Write one sentence instead of two using *who, which* or *where*.**
>
> 4 We climbed to the top of Mount Kea. It's 4205 metres above the sea.
> 5 My cousins live in France. They are scientists.
> 6 James visited the Amazon rainforest. There are a lot of different species there.

> **Student B**
>
> **Write one sentence instead of two using *who, which* or *where*.**
>
> 1 Hurricane Henry destroyed over 300 000 homes. It started on Tuesday night.
> 2 Dr Daniel Fahrenheit thought of a way of measuring temperature. He was born in 1686.
> 3 I was born in Bangladesh. There are often floods here.
>
> **Write these sentences in the passive.**
>
> 4 They told elderly people to take extra care.
> 5 They expect thick fog in this region tomorrow.
> 6 The floods are destroying the crops.

2 **Swap notebooks. Read and correct each other's sentences.**

3 **Check your answers with your teacher. You get one point for each correct sentence. The pair with the most points is the winner.**

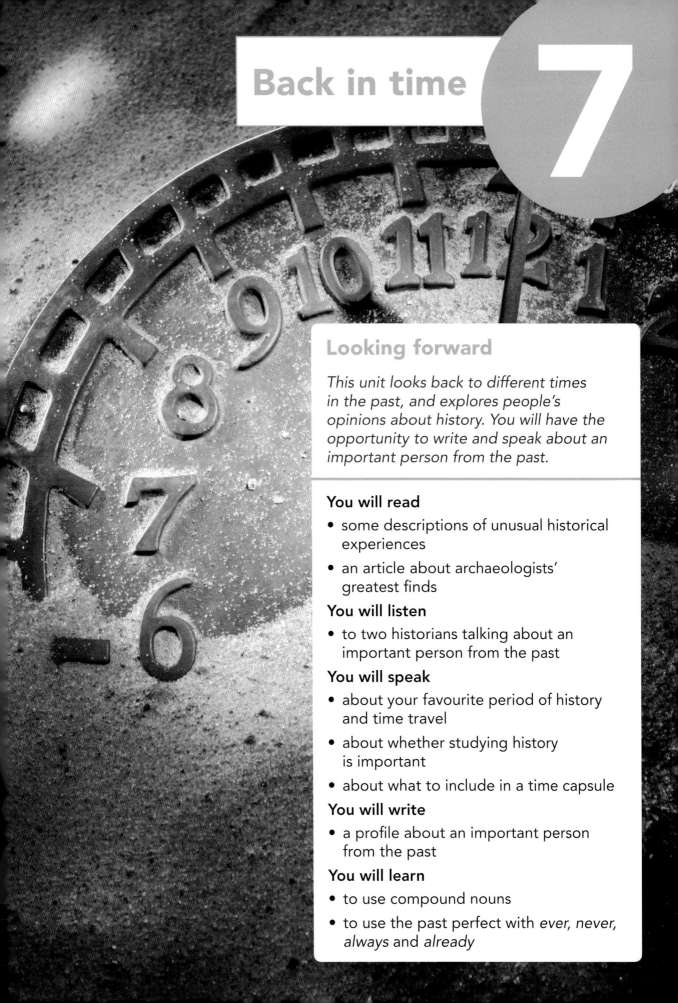

Back in time

7

Looking forward

This unit looks back to different times in the past, and explores people's opinions about history. You will have the opportunity to write and speak about an important person from the past.

You will read

- some descriptions of unusual historical experiences
- an article about archaeologists' greatest finds

You will listen

- to two historians talking about an important person from the past

You will speak

- about your favourite period of history and time travel
- about whether studying history is important
- about what to include in a time capsule

You will write

- a profile about an important person from the past

You will learn

- to use compound nouns
- to use the past perfect with *ever, never, always* and *already*

Bringing history alive

Vocabulary: talking about history

1 **Read and match the words in italics to the correct definition.**

My favourite ¹*period* of history is the ²*Middle Ages*. I love visiting historical ³*sites* and learning about ⁴*knights* in ⁵*battle*! I wouldn't have wanted to live then, but it would be great to visit in a time machine!

Last weekend, I went to a ⁶*virtual reality* ⁷*exhibition* about Ancient Egypt. I think it was the best exhibition I've ever been to! I felt like I was looking at real ⁸*mummies* in real ⁹*ancient* ¹⁰*tombs*.

a   a situation produced by a computer that seems almost real

b   the period of European history between the end the Roman Empire in 476 BCE and about 1500 CE

c   an event where interesting things are shown

d   a length of time

e   very old

f   places where something happens

g   a violent fight between groups of people

h   a dead body that was preserved long ago by being rubbed with special oils and wrapped in cloth

i   a stone grave where the body of a dead person is placed

j   in the past, a special type of soldier who rode a horse

2 **Discuss.**

- What's your favourite period of history and why? Would you like to have lived then? Why? / Why not?
- Where would you visit in a time machine and why?
- Have you ever been to an exhibition about history? What did you see and do?
- Have you ever been to a virtual reality exhibition? If you have, what was it like? If you haven't, would you like to? Why? / Why not?

> ### Language tip
> When you learn a new word, check the dictionary to see if there are any other words formed from this word. For example, the noun *history* is the root word for the adjective *historical* (about the past) and the noun *historian* (person who studies history).

talk about experiences and express opinions

Reading: some feelings about history

1 Read texts 1–3 below and match to photos a–c.

a    b    c

1 I used to find history really boring … But then I spent the night at a museum! It was so exciting being there at night-time! There was an exhibition about Ancient Egypt, and we explored an Egyptian tomb by moonlight. I felt like the mummies were watching me as I lay in my sleeping bag! I didn't feel scared, but I'm glad I wasn't alive then. I want to find out more about Ancient Egypt now. I wonder what sort of people were made into mummies.

Mark, 14, USA

2 I've always loved history, so my grandmother bought me this amazing new app for my birthday. It takes you back in time! When you visit a famous historical site, you can look at it through a virtual reality headset. This shows you what the site used to look like in the past. I went back to the Great Fire of London yesterday! The houses were burning right before my eyes. It was frightening and much more realistic than a film. Now, I want to find out more about it – for example, how did the Great Fire of London start?

Tim, 15, United Kingdom

3 I've always quite liked history, so last weekend we visited an old castle. There were lots of people dressed as knights from the Middle Ages. They fought a battle on the castle walls. It was very exciting, but also a bit scary. It made me feel glad that I'm alive now! Now I want to learn a lot more about that period. I wonder what it was like to be a knight in the Middle Ages …

Jan, 14, Germany

Language tip
Watch out for words that sound the same but have different spellings for different meanings, for example, *night* and *knight*, or *right* and *write*. Find examples of these in the text.

2 Read again and choose the correct option, a, b or c.

1   a   Mark spent the night in Egypt.

     b   Mark spent the night in a museum.

     c   Mark spent the night finding out about how mummies were made.

2   a   Tim saw the Great Fire of London come to life in a film.

     b   Tim saw a real fire at a famous historical site in London.

     c   Tim saw the Great Fire of London come to life in a virtual reality app.

3   a   Jan dressed up as a knight in a battle.

     b   Jan watched people dressed up as knights in a battle.

     c   Jan read a book about knights in a battle.

3 Read texts 1–3 on page 75 again and match the beginnings and ends of the sentences.

1 Mark   a didn't use to like history, but now he does.

2 Tim   b wanted to find out more about history after their experiences.

3 Jan   c were both frightened by their historical experiences.

4 Tim and Jan   d are both glad that they are alive now and not then.

5 Mark and Jan   e has always liked history.

6 Mark, Tim and Jan   f didn't use to mind history, but now he wants to learn more about it.

Use of English: compound nouns

1 Read the *Language tip* and find another five examples of compound nouns in the texts on page 75.

2 Write five new sentences with the compound nouns you have found.

> *When I woke up, the **moonlight** was coming through my bedroom window.*

3 Read your sentences to your partner, but don't say the compound noun. Can they guess what it is from the rest of the sentence?

Language tip
Compound nouns are nouns that are made of two or more words. They can be written as one word (*moonlight*), two words (*sleeping bag*) or hyphenated words (*night-time*).

Speaking: pronunciation of compound nouns

1 🔊 **7A** Listen to the compound nouns and mark the stress. What part of compound nouns do we stress?

> Last **weekend**, it was my **birthday**. **Everybody** was so kind to me. My **grandfather** gave me a new **basketball** and my **stepbrother** gave me a new **skateboard**!

2 In pairs, take turns to read the text in Activity 1 using the correct pronunciation of the compound nouns.

3 Complete the sentences about you using the correct pronunciation of the compound nouns.

1 Last weekend, I …

2 On my birthday, I want to …

3 Sometimes, I like to …

4 I think that football is …

Talking about people from the past

1 How much do you know about King Tutankhamun? Choose the correct answers. If you don't know the answer, then guess!

1 Where did King Tutankhamun come from?

   a   Rome   b   China   c   Egypt

2 Which century was he alive in?

   a   1300s BCE   b   1400s BCE   c   1400s CE

2 (7B) Listen to two podcasts and check your answers to Activity 1.

3 (7B) Read the *Listening tip* and copy the table below. Then listen again and complete the missing information for each historian. Which points do they agree on? Which do they disagree on?

King Tutankhamun	
Historian 1 says that:	**Historian 2 says that:**
He was born in [1]_____ BCE.	He was born in [7]_____ BCE.
He was king for [2]_____ years.	He was king for [8]_____ years.
He was buried with over [3]_____ objects.	He was buried with over [9]_____ objects.
His tomb was found in [4]_____ by [5]_____	His tomb was found in [10]_____ by [11]_____
Scientists think the King died because of a [6]_____	Scientists think the King died because of a [12]_____

Listening tip

Don't be confused if you hear people disagreeing with each other or even themselves. This is a natural part of speaking and if you are starting to recognise these differences, then it means you are becoming a better listener!

4 What are the historians' opinions of King Tutankhamun? Choose the correct options and explain your answers.

The historians agree that King Tutankhamun is one of the most [1][famous / important] people in history. But they disagree about whether he is one of the most [2][famous / important].

5 Why do you think that historians sometimes have different opinions about what happened in the past?

Listening: useful vocabulary

Match the words from the recording with the correct definition.

argue   bury   lie (v)   object (n)   bone   archaeologist

1   one of the hard, white parts inside your body
2   a person who studies the past by looking for old things in the ground
3   put something in the ground and cover it up
4   disagree with someone about something
5   a thing
6   be in a flat position on a surface

Use of English: past perfect with *never, ever, always* and *already*

1 (7C)) Listen to two students talking about the podcasts and write down the missing words.

Leanne: Hey, Simone, ¹ _____ of King Tutankhamun before we listened to those two podcasts?

Simone: Yes, I had. I ² _____ about him at school. What about you?

Leanne: I knew about his tomb, but I ³ _____ about his death before today. The two historians said completely different things about how he died! I ⁴ _____ that historians knew the facts about everything in the past!

Simone: Well, it was such a long time ago. Maybe we will never know the truth about what really happened in history.

2 Look at the examples in Activity 1 and complete the grammar rules.

1   We use the past perfect to talk about something that happened [before / after] something else happened in the past.
2   We form the past perfect with [*had* / *have*] + past participle.
3   We often use the past perfect with *ever, never, already* and *always*. These adverbs go just [before / after] the past participle.

3 Write these sentences in the past perfect.

1   [you / ever / learn] about knights in the Middle Ages before we studied it in history?
2   [We / never / visit] this historical site until last February.
3   Sarah didn't want to come to the exhibition because [she / already / try] the virtual reality app.
4   [They / always / want] to visit King Tutankhamun's tomb, so they visited last month.

deduce the meaning of vocabulary; past perfect simple forms in narrative

Writing: a profile

1 You are going to write a profile about a person from the past. Choose somebody you think was important or interesting.

2 Answer the questions to write a plan.

> *Paragraph 1*
> - What is his / her name?
> - Where did he / she come from?
> - When was he / she born? When did he / she die?
>
> *Paragraph 2*
> - What did he / she do in his / her life?
> - What is he / she mostly remembered for today?
>
> *Paragraph 3*
> - Why do you think that they are important?

3 Write your profile.

4 Read your work and ask yourself the following questions:
- Have I spelled all the words correctly?
- Have I missed out any punctuation?
- Have I used full sentences?
- Have I used three paragraphs?
- Have I got an interesting first and last sentence?

Speaking: thinking about history

1 Simone said, "Well, it was such a long time ago. Maybe we will never know the truth about what really happened in history." Do you agree with her? Explain your answer.

2 Read and discuss.

> *If you don't know history, then you don't know anything. You are a leaf that doesn't know it is part of a tree.*
> Michael Crichton, writer

> *History is just lies that people agree on.*
> Napoleon Bonaparte, ruler of France, early 19th century

Speaking tip

If you hear yourself make a mistake when you're speaking, don't worry! It's fine to say something again to correct yourself, but don't let it stop you from talking!

- Do you agree or disagree with these opinions? Explain your answers.
- Do you think it's important to learn about history? Why? / Why not?

Focus on History

Archaeologists' greatest finds

1 Discuss.

- Do you think the work of archaeologists is important? Why? / Why not?
- What difficulties do you think archaeologists face in their work?
- What skills do you think you need to be a good archaeologist?
- Would you like to be an archaeologist? Why? / Why not?

2 Read quickly and match pictures 1–4 with texts a–d.

1

2

3

4

a **King Tutankhamun's tomb**

Howard Carter was a British archaeologist who spent nearly 31 years looking for King Tutankhamun's tomb. Finally, on 4 November 1922, he found the tomb in a valley between two hills. When the tomb was opened on 26 November 1922, Carter said that it was full of 'wonderful things', including the mummy of the king inside a gold coffin. There were also thousands of special objects that Ancient Egyptians thought would be useful. There were gold **statues**, jewellery, clothes, toys, games, objects used for cooking, and musical instruments. King Tutankhamun died in around 1346 BCE. All the objects in his tomb helped historians to learn a lot about what life used to be like in Egypt at that time.

b

THE CITY OF POMPEII

In 1748, archaeologists started **digging** in southern Italy, looking for the **ruins** of a great Roman city, Pompeii. A huge volcano buried this city in volcanic rock in 79 CE. Underneath, however, Pompeii was kept almost exactly as it had been 2000 years before. Buildings were still standing, objects were lying on the streets, and even the bones of the people who had died in the volcano were found 'frozen in time'. Historians have learned a huge amount about daily Roman life from the ruins of Pompeii.

c

THE TERRACOTTA ARMY

In 1974, workers were digging a well near the city of Xi'an in China. They made one of the greatest finds in the world – a **soldier** made of terracotta, ready for battle. They told the Chinese government, who sent archaeologists to the site. Thousands more soldiers were found, all with different faces, as well as horses, all made of terracotta clay. The terracotta **army** had been made for the tomb of the first **emperor** of China in 209 BCE, and it has taught historians a lot about fighting and daily life in China during that period.

d

RICHARD III'S BONES

In 2013, the bones of King Richard III of England were found underneath a car park in the city of Leicester in the United Kingdom. King Richard had been killed in battle in 1485. Archaeologists learned new information about King Richard by studying his bones. They discovered that he probably had blue eyes and that he had died because he was hit on the head. They also found that King Richard had a problem with his back, which historians at the time he was alive had written about. Richard's bones were buried again in 2015 in Leicester Cathedral, in a large tomb.

3 **Answer the questions.**

1   What objects did archaeologists find in each site?
2   What did archaeologists learn from each find?

4 **Match the words in bold in the text with the correct definition.**

1   making a hole in the ground
2   a large group of soldiers who fight on land
3   a man who rules a group of countries
4   big models of things, usually of people or animals, often made of stone
5   somebody in an army
6   parts of a building that remain after the rest is destroyed

5 **Discuss.**

● How do you think the archaeologists felt when they made their finds?
● Which of these finds do you think is the most important and why?
● Which site would you most like to visit and why?

Project: make a time capsule

You are going to work in groups to plan your own time capsule.

1 Choose six objects to put in your time capsule. Choose things that will help people of the future understand what your life is like today. You can use some of the ideas from the box below or think of your own.

> ### Language tip
> A *time capsule* is a container for storing a number of objects, which are chosen because they are typical of that time. The time capsule is then buried for people to dig up at some time in the future.

a form of technology		a newspaper	
a book	a photo	a toy	some art
some music	some money	some clothes	

2 Draw or find simple pictures of the things that you have chosen and stick them on a poster. Write a few sentences to explain why you have chosen each object.

3 Write a letter together to the person in the future, who will open the time capsule, telling them about your lives now. You can talk about some of the things in the box below or think of your own ideas.

school	free time activities	music, film, TV preferences	fashions	travel

4 Stick the letter onto the poster and prepare it for display.

5 Share information about your time capsule with the rest of the class. Listen and ask questions.

- Which group included the most unusual object?
- Which group included the most interesting piece of information about the present time in their letter?

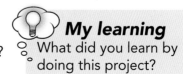

My learning
What did you learn by doing this project?

Who am I?

8

56"78901

(8100)1

23456(21)

1 III234

Looking forward

This unit considers what makes us individuals and the factors that influence our identity.

You will read

- about different people's personal identities
- an extract from a novel, *I Will Always Write Back* by Caitlin Alifirenka and Martin Ganda

You will listen

- to an interview with a set of twins
- to someone talking about the interview

You will speak

- about your identity and character

You will write

- an email to a new pen pal, telling them about yourself

You will learn

- to use prepositions after adjectives
- to use questions ending with prepositions
- to use reported speech for statements

III23456"78901 (8100)1 23456(21)12345678

0 12 34567 89012 8

Talking about yourself

1 Which of the adjectives in the box would you use to describe yourself and why? What other adjectives would you use?

> warm   calm
>
> generous   confident
>
> independent   creative

2 Discuss.

- What are the three best things about you?
- What are the three worst things about you?

3 Choose the correct options.

1 Your *character* is all the things that make you:
   a the same as other people
   b different from other people
   c happy.

2 Your *identity* is who:
   a your friends think you are
   b your family want you to be
   c you are.

3 Your *nationality* is being:
   a part of a club
   b a citizen of a city
   c a citizen of a country.

4 Your *gender* is whether you are:
   a old or young
   b male or female
   c tall or short.

5 The *media* is:
   a TV, newspapers, radio and so on
   b what you get if you win
   c what you take when you're ill.

1 **Read and complete the chat room posts with the words in the box.**

family   media   nationality and language   gender   friends

Who are you? Tell us what makes YOU who YOU are, and why!

My name is Marco and I come from Italy. I think my identity comes partly from my [1] _____ . I grew up here, and all my experiences here have made me the person that I am today. I'm very proud of the fact that I'm Italian and that I speak Italian. That's who I am! *Marco, 15, Italy*

For me, one of the most important things about my identity is my [2] _____ . Some people say it doesn't make any difference whether you are male or female. I'm always amazed at this idea. In my opinion, women are often friendlier than men and men are often more competitive than women. That's my experience, anyway. *Saira, 14, Canada*

I think that I get my identity mostly from my [3] _____ . My parents and my brother and sister made me who I am. I'm very keen on art and I'm creative – I get that from my mum. I'm also generous – that's why I'm similar to my dad. *Lucien, 15, Sweden*

I think that the [4] _____ has played an enormous part in making me who I am. For example, I'm fond of rock music, I watch adventure films and I read the newspapers online every day. These things have helped me to become independent, because I now know which things I like and which things I don't like. *Arjun, 16, India*

I think my [5] _____ are really important to my identity. My relationships with the people around me have helped to make me who I am. I used to feel really anxious about school, but I'm much more confident now, and that's all because of my classmates! *Kalifa, 13, Kenya*

2 **What makes you who you are? Think about the words in the box in Activity 1. To answer the question, rank them from most important to least important.**

3 **Read again and answer the questions.**
1   Who thinks their character is similar to their parents'?
2   Who feels proud of where they come from?
3   Whose attitude to school has changed?
4   Who feels confident about the things they like?
5   Who considers that there are differences between men and women?

Writing: spelling patterns

Read the *Spelling tip*. Think of other words that you know that follow these spelling patterns, or look for new words. Check the meaning of new words in a dictionary.

- words that end in –ent: confid<u>ent</u>, independ<u>ent</u> …
- words that end in –ous: gener<u>ous</u>, enorm<u>ous</u> …
- words that end in –ence: experi<u>ence</u>, differ<u>ence</u> …

Spelling tip

When you learn new vocabulary, watch out for patterns of words that are spelled in a similar way, for example:

confid<u>ent</u> and independ<u>ent</u>
gener<u>ous</u> and enorm<u>ous</u>
experi<u>ence</u> and differ<u>ence</u>

Use of English: adjectives + prepositions

1 **Read the *Language tip*. Copy and complete the sentences from the chat room posts with the correct prepositions.**

1 I'm very <u>proud</u> _____ the fact that I am Italian.
2 I'm always <u>amazed</u> _____ this idea.
3 I'm very <u>keen</u> _____ art.
4 I'm <u>similar</u> _____ my dad.
5 I'm <u>fond</u> _____ rock music.
6 I used to feel really <u>anxious</u> _____ school.

2 **Say your own sentences using the adjectives + prepositions from Activity 1.**

Language tip

Some adjectives are followed by prepositions, for example, *proud of*. It's best to learn these as whole phrases so that you remember to use the correct preposition. In informal written English and in spoken English, we often end a question with a preposition: *What are you most proud of?*

Use of English: questions ending with prepositions

1 (8A) **Read the *Language tip* again. Make questions, adding prepositions after the adjectives. Then listen and check.**

1 What / you / be / most / proud?
2 What sport / you / be / keen / most?
3 Who / most / you / be / similar?
4 Who / you / most / be / fond?
5 What / you / feel / anxious / most?

> *What are you most proud of?*

> *I'm most proud of the fact I can play the piano.*

2 (8A) **Listen again and answer the questions.**

1 Do we stress prepositions when they are in the middle of the sentence?
2 Do we stress prepositions when they are at the end of a question?

3 **Ask and answer the questions in pairs. Remember to use the correct stress.**

Finding your identity

Listening: what it's like to be a twin

1 Read about the radio programme and match the words in italics to the definitions below.

> Listen to Elena Gonzalez talking to ¹*identical* ²*twins*, Sara and Nadia, about how they found their own ³*separate* identities and how people got to know them as ⁴*individuals*.

a apart and not connected to anything else

b two people who were born at the same time to the same mother

c exactly the same

d one person

2 Discuss.

- Do you know any twins? Are they similar to or different from each other?
- Why do you think it's difficult for twins to be known as individuals?
- What do you think Sara and Nadia might say about how they found their separate identities?

3 **8B** Listen once. Did you predict correctly in Activity 2?

4 **8B** Listen again and choose the correct options.

1 Which twin was born first?

  a Sara   b Nadia   c They don't know.

2 What did the twins' parents encourage them to do?

  a to look identical   b to have identical personal identities

  c to have separate personal identities

3 What two things helped the twins to become independent?

  a wearing the same clothes and doing the same things

  b living apart and having different jobs

  c having different jobs and feeling confident

5 Discuss. Give reasons for your answers.

1 Do Sara and Nadia like being twins? Do they want to be known as twins or individuals?

2 Why did they find it difficult to find their own separate identities when they were at school? Why did this become easier after they left home?

3 How do they feel about their separate identities now? Are they as close now as they were when they were children?

listen for specific information and recognise speakers' opinions   87

Use of English: reported speech

1 **(8C)** **You're going to hear somebody talking about Nadia and Sara's radio interview. Listen and write down the missing words.**

"I listened to this really interesting interview on the radio last week with a set of identical twins, Sara and Nadia. Sara said that ¹ _____ which of ² _____ first all those years ³ _____ and she said that ⁴ _____ parents ⁵ _____ in the same clothes either. Nadia said that ⁶ _____ very different jobs and ⁷ _____ important for personal identity. Sara told us that ⁸ _____ closer than ever and that ⁹ _____ on holiday together ¹⁰ _____!"

2 **Look at the words that you wrote in Activity 1 and compare them with what Sara and Nadia actually said below. Then copy and complete the rules below with the words from the box.**

"We don't know which of us was born first all those years ago!"

"Our parents never dressed us in the same clothes."

"We also do very different jobs and this is important when it comes to personal identity."

"We're closer than ever! In fact, we're going on holiday together tomorrow!"

| pronouns | told | time and place phrases | said | tenses | demonstratives |

1 When we use reported speech, we usually change:
   a the _____ by moving them back one step, so, for example, the present simple in direct speech becomes the past simple in reported speech.
   b _____, for example *I* and *you* become *he* or *she* and *we* becomes *they*.
   c _____, for example *this* becomes *that*.
   d _____, for example *tomorrow* becomes *the next day* or *the following day* and *here* becomes *there*.

2 We use the verb _____ when we say who somebody is talking to and we use the verb _____ when we don't.

3 **Write these sentences using reported speech.**

1 Nadia said, "We love being twins, but we don't want that to be the only thing that makes us who we are."

2 She went on to say, "We're lucky really."

3 "Our parents never told us," said Sara.

4 She also said, "I think it was quite difficult when we were at school."

Punctuation tip

Note the use of speech marks and the position of the comma when writing direct speech.

Nadia said, "We love being twins, but we don't want that to be the only thing that makes us who we are."

"Our parents never told us," said Sara.

Speaking: checking what somebody said

1 **Read the *Speaking tip* and match the phrases to the uses.**

1 *"I'm sorry, I didn't understand that. Could you say it again using different words, please?"*

2 *"Excuse me, but I didn't catch that. Would you mind saying it again more slowly?"*

3 *"So, what you're saying is … / So, what you mean is …"*

a If you didn't understand because somebody spoke too quickly.

b If you want to repeat back what somebody said to make sure that you've understood it correctly.

c If you didn't understand the words that someone used.

> ### Speaking tip
> If you don't understand what someone has said to you, then don't be afraid to stop the conversation and ask them to say it again. If you want to check that you have understood correctly, then try repeating what they said back to them in your own words.

2 **Discuss in pairs. Use the expressions from Activity 1 if you don't understand something.**

Do you think your identity is different when you speak English from when you speak your own language? Why?

Writing: an email about yourself

1 **Choose the correct option.**

A *pen pal* is a friend:

a who likes pens   b you write to   c who sells pens.

2 **Read Paulo's email and write a reply. Use the same email layout as he does and answer the questions he asks in the last paragraph.**

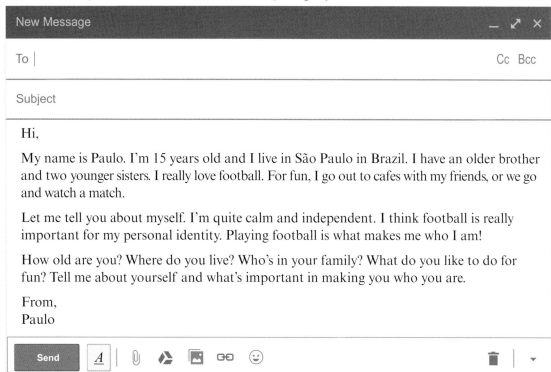

New Message   — ⤢ ✕

To | Cc Bcc

Subject

Hi,

My name is Paulo. I'm 15 years old and I live in São Paulo in Brazil. I have an older brother and two younger sisters. I really love football. For fun, I go out to cafes with my friends, or we go and watch a match.

Let me tell you about myself. I'm quite calm and independent. I think football is really important for my personal identity. Playing football is what makes me who I am!

How old are you? Where do you live? Who's in your family? What do you like to do for fun? Tell me about yourself and what's important in making you who you are.

From,
Paulo

Send   *A* ⬚ ⟁ ⬚ ⊖ ☺   🗑 ▾

check what someone has said; use style and register and appropriate layout in writing   89

Focus on Literature

Non-fiction

1 **Answer the questions.**

- Have you ever read a book that was based on a true story? Do you think this makes a book more or less interesting? Why?

- What do you think we can learn by talking to people from different cultures?

- Find Pennsylvania (USA) and Mutare (Zimbabwe) on a map. Do you think a girl from Pennsylvania and a boy from Mutare would have anything in common? Why? / Why not?

2 **Read the start of the book *I Will Always Write Back* by Martin Ganda and Caitlin Alifirenka and choose the correct option.**

Martin and Caitlin:

a are old friends   **b** have never met before   **c** met last week.

Caitlin

*I'd never heard of Zimbabwe. But something about the way the name looked up on the blackboard interested me. It was different, and difficult to **pronounce**. It was also the last country in a long list that Mrs Miller had written. She asked each student in my seventh-grade English class to **pick** a place for a pen pal program our school was starting that year.*

I didn't know then – how could I have? – but that moment would change my life.

*Before then, I was a typical twelve-year-old American girl, far more interested in what I should wear to school than what I might learn there. I thought most kids, wherever they lived, had lives similar to mine. And while I **imagined** that Zimbabwe was different from Pennsylvania, where I grew up, I had no idea how much …*

Our homework that night was to write a letter to our new pen pal.

I began: Hi, my name is Caitlin. I'm twelve years old. I live in Hatfield, Pennsylvania. I'm in the seventh grade. My brother Richie is in eleventh grade.

*I stopped. What else should I write to this person halfway across the world? I looked over my room for ideas and saw my collection of sports prizes won over the years, usually for good sportsmanship, as I was never the best player, or even very athletic. I **continued**.*

I play softball and soccer and field hockey. For fun, I like to go shopping at the mall on the weekend. I also like to go roller skating and bowling with my friends. And to eat pizza. What do you like to do for fun? And what is it like in Zimbabwe? Sincerely, Caitlin.

When I gave my letter to Mrs Miller the following day, I felt excited, like this was the start of something big.

Martin

Mrs Jarai came into our classroom, smiling.

"Class, I have pen pal letters from America!" she said in a happy voice. It was mid-October and towards the end of our school year, so this was a welcome surprise.

Everyone started talking – we all knew and loved America … I wanted to know what kids my age were like in this country that was a long way away.

Mrs Jarai only had ten letters – and there were fifty students in our classroom. I was one of the lucky ones … Mrs Jarai handed me the first letter and asked me to read it out loud. We learned English in school but I spoke our local language with my family and friends. I knew how to speak English but used it in only in this class, so the words felt funny in my mouth. I tried to **copy** the voices I had heard on the radio and television.

"Hello, my name is Caitlin," I began. It was such a strange name that everyone laughed.

I had never heard of Pennsylvania, and had a difficult time pronouncing it. But then I got to the part where she listed the sports she played and smiled: we had something in common. I played soccer daily with my friends but had never heard of field hockey and was not sure how to say the word.

Mrs Jarai told those of us who had gotten letters to write a reply and bring it back the following day. I always loved homework, but this felt more important than any regular school work: I had a new friend in America.

That night I wrote my letter by the light of the fire. I did not want to ask her too many questions. Instead I wrote a basic letter, using hers as my guide. I told her what grade I was in, and the names of my brothers and sisters. I told her that I loved to play soccer, and that I really hoped we'd continue to write each other. I **promised** her I would not let her down, and I hoped she would do the same.

---

3 **Read again and answer the questions.**

1. How did Caitlin feel when she was writing the letter to Martin?
2. How did Martin feel when he received the letter?
3. What did they have in common?
4. How did Martin feel about writing his letter?
5. Do you think they will carry on writing to each other? Why? / Why not?
6. How would you describe the characters of Caitlin and Martin from reading the start of the book?

4 **What do the verbs in bold mean? Make sentences of your own with these verbs.**

5 **Discuss.**

- "I knew how to speak English but used it in only in this class, so the words felt funny in my mouth." Do you ever feel like Martin when you are speaking English? Give details.

- "What else should I write to this person halfway across the world?" What would you write to a pen pal on the other side of the world? Would you like to receive a letter from somebody who lives a long way away? Why? / Why not?

Language tip

American English is different from British English. There are differences in:

- vocabulary, for example, they say *soccer* instead of *football* and *mall* instead of *shopping centre*

- grammar, for example, they say *those of us who had **gotten** letters* instead of *those of us who had **got** letters*

- spelling, for example, *program* instead of *programme*.

Project: make a display about your class – *Who are we?*

You are going to make a display about all the people in your class.

1 Work in pairs. Find out about your partner. Use the ideas below and add some of your own.

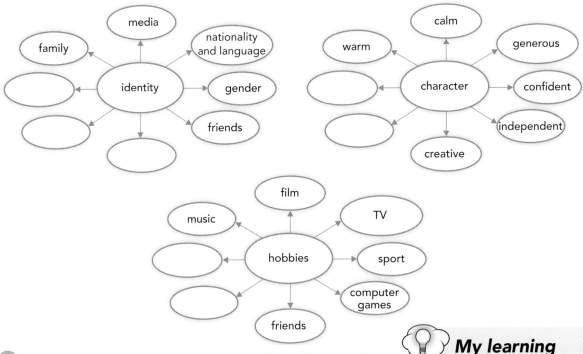

2 Take a photograph of your partner that relates to the information you now know about them.

My learning
What did you learn by doing this project?

3 Write about your partner. Include information about:

- their identity
- their character
- their hobbies.

4 Read and edit your work. Check your spelling and your grammar. Then put your photos and texts together and make a big display about your class.

5 Read your display and compare. Are you all different? Are some people similar?

interact to achieve a shared outcome; describe people

Mid-year review

1 **Discuss.**

- How has the world changed since your grandparents were children?
- Would you rather have grown up then or now?

2 **Read quickly and complete the sentences.**

1 The most important things for Suzanne's personal identity are her ____ and ____ .
2 The most important things for Martine's personal identity are her ____ and ____ .

Personal identity, then and now

My name is Suzanne, I am 75 years old and I come from France. The most important thing about my identity is my nationality. When we were young, we were taught at school to love our country. I was always told by my parents that I should be proud to be French. I have never forgotten this and I still feel proud today. I also think that our language, which is French of course, is important.

Things are different for young people today. My granddaughter Martine, who is 15, speaks three languages, whereas I only speak French. (She is translating this for me now!) When I was her age, I had never travelled abroad and I didn't know anything about the world. Last week she returned from China and I told her she was very lucky to have such wonderful opportunities!

My name is Martine, I am 15 years old and I am French. Although I love my country and my language, I don't think these things are really important in making me who I am today. I think that I get my identity mostly from my gender. I am very proud to be a young woman and I know that I am being given many opportunities that my grandmother never had. I also think that my friends are important for my personal identity. They have helped to make me into the person I am today. I'm not sure who I would be without them!

3 **Read again and answer the questions.**

1 What was Suzanne taught at school?
2 How many languages does Suzanne speak?
3 How does Martine compare her life with Suzanne's life?
4 Why are Martine's friends important to her?

Use of English: language in context

Look again at the text on page 93. Find the following and answer the questions.

1 Two verbs in the present perfect tense. (See page 32.) Why are they used in these sentences?

2 A verb in the past perfect tense. (See page 78.) Why did they use this tense?

3 Two present passives. (See pages 53 and 67.) What two forms of present passive are used and why?

4 Two past simple passives. (See page 53) Why is the past simple passive used?

5 Two conjunctions of contrast. (See page 44.) In each case, why did they choose to use this type of conjunction?

6 Two relative clauses that add information. (See page 65.) Which relative pronouns are used and why?

7 An example of reported speech. (See page 88.) What were the exact words she said?

8 Two compound nouns. (See page 76.) What are the two nouns in each compound noun?

Vocabulary: words in context

1 Read the sentences about extreme weather and the planet. Choose the best word to complete them.

1 Asia is the largest ____ in the world.
   a continent   b country   c ocean

2 There are millions of different species in the Amazon ____ .
   a wetforest   b waterforest   c rainforest

3 There's a ____ weather warning about the hurricane.
   a severe   b serious   c bad

4 Temperatures have been very high during this heat ____ .
   a wave   b weather   c time

2 Read the sentences about describing people. Choose the best word to complete them.

1 James is very ____ because he bought me my lunch and my train ticket.
   a calm   b generous   c confident

2 Sophia doesn't need anyone else's help because she's very ____ .
   a warm   b amazed   c independent

3 I look ____ my brother – we both have blonde hair and blue eyes. He's taller than me, though.
   a different from   b identical to   c similar to

4 He's ____ his exams – he's nervous and worried about what will happen.
   a anxious about   b proud of   c keen on

Speaking: explaining your opinion

Discuss in groups. Listen to what others have to say and give your opinions.

- What's the best film ever made? Why?
- What's the best sport in the world? Why?
- Is school important? Why? / Why not?
- Are e-readers better than books? Why? / Why not?
- What's the most exciting extreme place on the planet? Why?
- What period in history would you most like to visit and why?

Use these phrases to help you:

I think …	*In my opinion …*	*I believe …*	*It seems to me that …*
I feel this way because ….	*I think this because …*	*This is my opinion because …*	
I couldn't agree more!	*Exactly! That's my view too.*		
I agree but …	*That's a good point but …*		

Use of English: correction competition

Read the instructions for the competition. Work in pairs.

- Read the sentences. Four are correct but four are incorrect.
- You get one mark for each correct sentence you find.
- You get two marks for each incorrect sentence that you can correct.
- The winners are the pair with the most points.

1   Gabriel suggested go to the cinema on Friday.
2   Forests are been destroyed all over the world at the moment.
3   I play football slightly better than my brother.
4   Travelling to school isn't easy for some people.
5   On what age should you start learning about history?
6   I feel really disappointing with my exam results.
7   He lost his book. That's why he's unhappy.
8   I listened to the weather forecast. I checked the forecast online, as well.

1 8D) **Listen to the people talking. Read the questions and choose the best answers.**

1   What sort of films does Yasmin like best?

a

b

c

2   What's the most extreme weather that Keira has experienced?

a

b
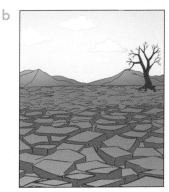

c

3   Where does Sam most want to go?

a

b

c

2 8D) **Listen again and answer the questions.**

1   Why does Yasmin find sci-fi films interesting?
2   What sort of films does she find boring?
3   When did Keira see extreme weather?
4   What happened as a result of the extreme weather?
5   Why is this a hard question for Sam?
6   Why does he decide on the place he chooses in the end?

Use of English: rewording

Read the A sentences. Complete the B sentences so that they have the same meaning.

Use no more than three words.

1 A Aliya can run slightly faster than Harriet.

   B Harriet can't run _____ Aliya.

2 A Nina's team won the basketball tournament.

   B The basketball tournament _____ Nina's team.

3 A Mateo and Diego are identical twins. They come from Colombia.

   B Mateo and Diego, _____ Colombia, are identical twins.

4 A The children thought the film was terrifying.

   B The children were _____ by the film.

5 A "I have never read this book," said Leah.

   B Leah said that she _____ that book.

Speaking: expressing your opinion

1 Think about the following questions and make notes.

- What are the advantages of reading a book instead of watching a film?
- What are the disadvantages of reading a book instead of watching a film?
- Which activity do you prefer to do during your free time?

2 Discuss in small groups. Use the useful expressions from the box.

One advantage is …	*Another advantage is …*
One disadvantage is …	*Another disadvantage is …*
In my opinion, …	

Writing: expressing your opinion and developing arguments

What are the advantages and disadvantages of reading a book instead of watching a film?

1 Use your notes from *Speaking: expressing your opinion* to write a plan.

Paragraph 1 / Introduction: Introduce the question

Paragraph 3: Disadvantages

Paragraph 2: Advantages

Paragraph 4 / Conclusion: Your opinion

2 Write the essay. Use some of the useful expressions from the box above.

3 Read and edit your essay. Ask yourself these questions.

- Have I written a clear introduction?
- Are all the advantages in one paragraph and disadvantages in another?
- Have I reached a clear conclusion and given my opinion?

Reading: letter to a pen pal

1 Complete the email with one word in each space.

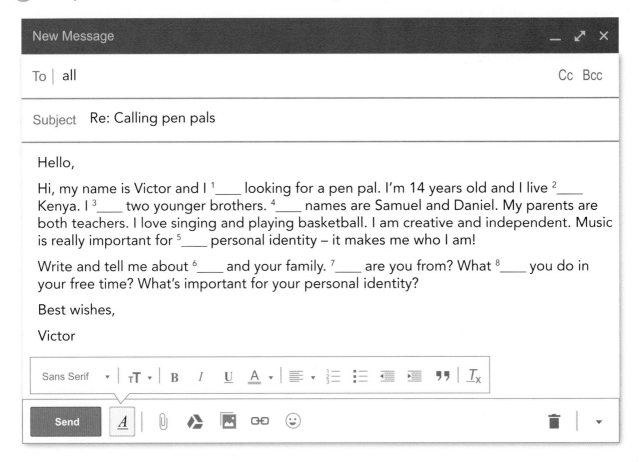

New Message   — ↗ ✕

To | all   Cc Bcc

Subject   Re: Calling pen pals

Hello,

Hi, my name is Victor and I ¹____ looking for a pen pal. I'm 14 years old and I live ²____ Kenya. I ³____ two younger brothers. ⁴____ names are Samuel and Daniel. My parents are both teachers. I love singing and playing basketball. I am creative and independent. Music is really important for ⁵____ personal identity – it makes me who I am!

Write and tell me about ⁶____ and your family. ⁷____ are you from? What ⁸____ you do in your free time? What's important for your personal identity?

Best wishes,

Victor

Sans Serif ▾ | ᴛT ▾ | B I U A ▾ | ≡ ▾ ⅓≡ ⋮≡ ◁ ▷ 𝟿𝟿 | Tₓ

Send A | 📎 ▲ 🖼 🔗 ☺   🗑 | ▾

2 Answer the questions.

1   What are Victor's brothers called?

2   What do his parents do?

3   What does he do in his free time?

4   How does he describe himself?

5   What's the most important thing in making him who he is?

Writing: an email

Write an email to reply to Victor.

- Use the same email format as he does.

- Answer the questions he asks in the last paragraph.

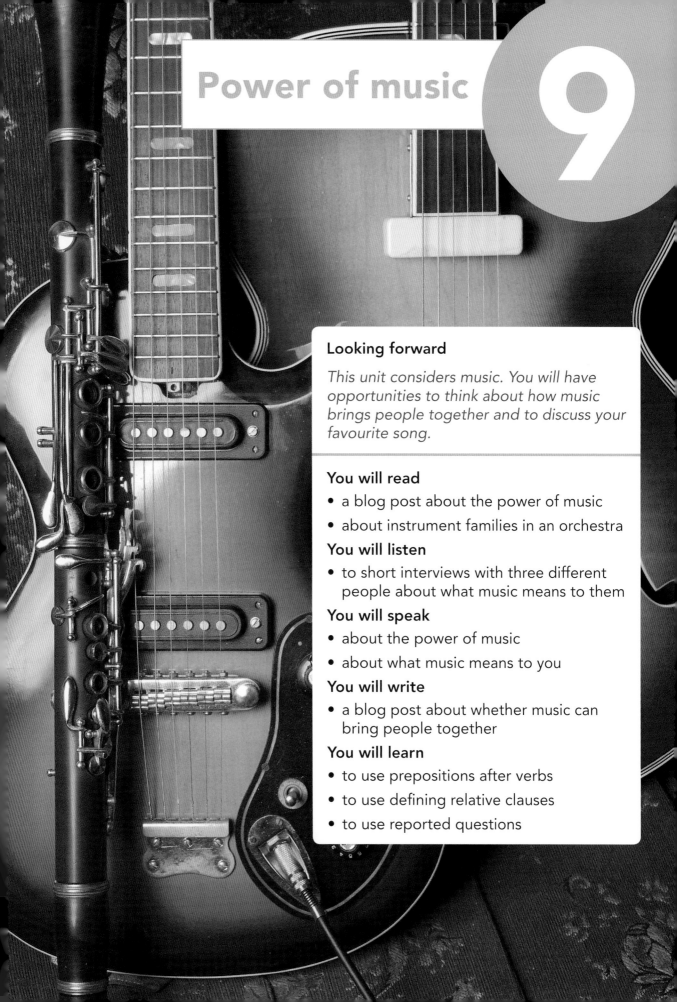

Power of music

9

Looking forward

This unit considers music. You will have opportunities to think about how music brings people together and to discuss your favourite song.

You will read
- a blog post about the power of music
- about instrument families in an orchestra

You will listen
- to short interviews with three different people about what music means to them

You will speak
- about the power of music
- about what music means to you

You will write
- a blog post about whether music can bring people together

You will learn
- to use prepositions after verbs
- to use defining relative clauses
- to use reported questions

Music and change

Language tip

The person who:

writes a *blog* is a *blogger*
makes *music* is a *musician*
plays a *piano* is a *pianist*
performs music is a *performer*.

 Discuss.

- Do you agree that music is powerful? Why? / Why not?
- Do you think that music can change the world? Why? / Why not?

 Read quickly and choose the correct option. You have one minute!

This blogger thinks that music ¹[is / isn't] powerful and thinks that it ²[can / can't] change the world.

Can music really change the world?

There are some people who say that music can't change the world … I disagree with this idea! I believe that we can use the power of music to make the world a better place. How can music do this? Let me tell you.

Firstly, music is an art form which is VERY LOUD! This means that it makes people sit up, **pay attention** and listen. For example, 1984 was the year when a group of musicians first came together to form the pop music group, Band Aid. Their famous song made a lot of noise, and also made a lot of money to help people in Africa who had nothing to eat.

In addition, music can communicate with people's feelings in a way that words can't. For instance, pianist Ludovico Einaudi wanted to make people care about the fact that the Arctic is in danger. So, he wrote and **performed** some beautiful music on his piano in the Arctic Ocean. This has made people care enough to do something about this important **environmental issue**.

What is more, music can be used to tell people about terrible things that are happening around the world. For example, musician and performer Emmanuel Jal has written music about what happened to him in the country where he was born, Sudan. His song *War Child* starts with the words: *I'm a war child / I believe I've **survived** for a reason. / To tell my story, to touch lives.* Emmanuel Jal has now helped a lot of **charities**.

To sum up, let's not just complain about **world problems**. Think about the people whose lives we can change. I dream about a better world – that's why we should play our music and sing our songs loudly, and hopefully make a difference to the world too!

3 **Read again and answer the questions.**

1 What was the name of the pop group that made a song for Africa?

2 What year did they make their song?

3 What part of the world was Ludovico Einaudi trying to help?

4 What instrument does he play?

5 Who wrote the song *War Child*?

6 Which country was he born in?

4 **Match the examples of expressions for presenting arguments to their uses.**

1 *for example ... / for instance ...*

2 *Firstly, ... / To start, ...*

3 *In addition, ... / What is more, ... / Additionally, ...*

4 *To sum up, ... / Finally, ... / In conclusion, ...*

a to introduce their first argument

b to finish their argument

c to introduce examples

d to introduce more arguments

5 **Look again at the blog post opposite and answer the questions.**

1 What three arguments does the blogger give to back up his opinion about the power of music?

2 Does he put different arguments in different paragraphs? What expressions does he use to introduce his arguments?

3 What examples does he use to back up each argument?

4 What expressions does he use to introduce his examples?

Reading tip

When a writer wants to tell a reader about something they feel strongly about, they should give details of their arguments to explain why they feel the way they do. These arguments are made stronger with examples or evidence.

6 **Discuss.**

● Do you agree or disagree with the blogger's opinion? Why?

● Do you think his arguments are strong? Why? / Why not?

● Do you think his examples are good? Why? / Why not?

Vocabulary: words in context

Match the words in bold in the article on page 100 with the correct definition.

1 did something in front of an audience
2 to do with the natural world
3 still existed after a difficult or dangerous time
4 watch and listen carefully
5 organisations that work for people who need help
6 an important subject that people are talking about

Use of English: verbs + prepositions

1 **Copy and complete the sentences from the blog post with the prepositions *with* or *about*.**

1 *I **disagree** _____ this idea!*
2 *Music makes people **care** _____ important issues.*

2 **Find two other verbs in the blog post that are followed by *with* and two verbs that are followed by *about*.**

> *I **disagree with** the idea that classical music is old-fashioned.*

3 **Write sentences of your own using the verbs + prepositions from Activities 1 and 2.**

Use of English: relative clauses

1 **Read the *Language tip*. Copy and complete the sentences from the blog post with the pronouns from the box.**

> ### Language tip
> We use a defining relative clause to give information that is essential to the meaning of the sentence.

which / that	when	who	why	where

1 There are some people _____ say that music can't change the world.
2 Firstly, music is an art form _____ is VERY LOUD!
3 1984 was the year _____ a group of musicians first came together to make the pop group Band Aid.
4 Emmanuel Jal has written music about what happened to him in the country _____ he was born.
5 That's _____ we should use the power of music to help!

2 **Match the relative pronouns to their use.**

1 who   a place
2 which / that   b time
3 where   c person
4 when   d reason
5 why   e thing

What does music mean to us?

Listening: talking about music

1 **Discuss.**

- Is music important to you? Why? / Why not?
- How does listening to music make you feel?

2 (9A) **Listen to Lin asking three people how they feel about music. How many of them say that music is important to them?**

3 (9A) **Listen again to each speaker and choose the correct answer.**

1 How does the first speaker say that music makes him feel?

   a It sometimes makes him happy and sometimes makes him sad.

   b It always makes him happy.

   c It doesn't really change the way he feels.

2 How does the second speaker think that music helps her students?

   a It helps them to relax and feel happy during lessons, so they learn more.

   b It helps them to remember and use grammar.

   c It helps them to learn new vocabulary.

3 Why does the third speaker think music is important?

   a Because music always makes her feel happy.

   b Because she can always find the right music for her mood.

   c Because it stops her from feeling embarrassed.

Vocabulary: feelings

1 **Copy and complete the adjectives from the recording, which describe feelings.**

relax ____   stress ____   lone ____   miser ____   cheer ____   embarrass ____

2 **Which of the feelings are happy and which are sad?**

listen to recognise speakers' opinions   103

Use of English: reported questions

1 **Copy and complete the questions that Lin asked.**

1 "____ you a music fan?"

2 "____ you like music or not?"

3 "What ____ music mean to you?"

4 "____ music important in your life?"

5 "____ music always been important or is it just recently?"

6 "What part ____ music play in your life?"

2 **Look again at the questions and group them into these three categories.**

1 *yes / no* questions   2 choice questions   3 question-word questions

3 **Look at the table showing reported questions, and compare them to the direct questions in Activity 1. Then match the sentence halves below to complete the grammar rules.**

yes / no questions	choice questions	question-word questions
Lin **asked** him **if** he was a music fan.	Lin **asked** her **if** he liked music or not.	Lin **asked** him **what** music meant to him.
Lin **asked** her **whether** music was important in her life.	Lin **asked** her **whether** music had always been important to her or if it was just recently.	Lin **asked** her **what** part music played in her life.

1 To report *yes / no* and choice questions,

2 To report question-word questions,

3 We make the same changes to tenses, pronouns and time words

a as we do in reported speech.

b we use *ask + if / whether*.

c we use *ask + question word*.

4 **Report these questions.**

1 Sarah asked Leah, "Do you like pop music?"

2 Pavlos asked me, "Does your brother listen to a lot of music?"

3 He asked them, "Do you listen to the radio or watch TV?"

4 Jared asked his mother, "Do you want the music loud or quiet?"

5 "What do you want to listen to?" Otis asked his friend.

6 Fred asked Lucilla, "Why do you like this song?"

Language tip

Remember that we don't change the tense in reported questions if the original statement is still true. For example:

She asked, "Which country is Munich in?"

She asked which country Munich is in.

Punctuation tip

Look at the punctuation used in direct questions. Don't forget to use speech marks and commas in the correct places in your writing.

Speaking: opinions about music

1 **Read the *Speaking tip*, then play a game in pairs!**

- Choose a word that has something to do with music. Don't tell your partner.

- Use the ideas in the *Speaking tip* to communicate the word to your partner. Don't say the word! Can your partner guess your word?

2 **Discuss these opinions from the recording. Do you agree or disagree? Why? If you forget a word that you want to use, try the ideas from the *Speaking tip*.**

- "*Music puts me in a good mood.*"
- "*Music is a great way of learning a language.*"
- "*Music makes me feel like I'm not alone.*"
- "*Music brings people together and that's brilliant.*"

Writing a blog post: *Can music bring people together*?

1 **You're going to write a blog post: *Can music bring people together*? First, write a plan.**

- Decide what your opinion is on this subject.

- Think of three good arguments to explain your opinion.

- Think of three examples to back up each of your arguments.

For example:

I think that music and singing in a group definitely bring people together. For example, at the Young Voices concerts, groups from all over the country meet and sing together.

Paragraph one	Introduction – state your opinion
Paragraph two	Point 1: Example 1:
Paragraph three	Point 2: Example 2:
Paragraph four	Point 3: Example 3:
Paragraph five	Conclusion – state your opinion again

2 **Write your blog post.**

3 **Read and edit your blog post, then share it with a partner.**

Speaking tip

If you can't remember an exact word when you are talking, try one of these ideas:

- use a more general word: if you can't remember *guitarist*, say *musician*.

- use a word that means the same thing: if you can't remember *loud*, say *noisy*.

- use a word that means the opposite: if you can't remember *loud*, say *not quiet*.

- describe the word: if you can't remember *MP3 player*, say *it's the thing you use to keep and listen to music*.

- give examples: if you can't remember *classical music*, say *for example, music by Beethoven, Bach or Vivaldi*.

My learning

Did you remember to use the useful phrases from the *Reading tip* on page 101 in your blog post?

Focus on Music

Instrument families in an orchestra

1 **Discuss.**

- Do you play a musical instrument? Do you play in an orchestra? Give details.
- Do you ever listen to orchestra music? Do you like it? Why? / Why not?

2 **Read quickly, then copy and complete the sentences below.**

An orchestra is divided into four different instrument families. Musical instruments belong to one of these families. The conductor is very important because this person tells the musicians when to play their parts.

Percussion
The percussion includes a lot of different instruments, some large and some small. You play a percussion instrument by hitting it or shaking it. These instruments often keep the rhythm of the music.

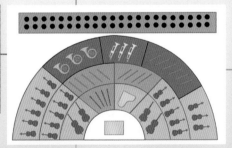

Brass
The loudest of the orchestra instruments, you play these by blowing into them in a special way. You press the keys to change the sounds.

Woodwind
You play these instruments by blowing into them. There are holes in the instruments, and you get different sounds by covering and uncovering holes with your fingers or by pressing the keys.

Strings
The string family is the largest in the orchestra – usually more than half of all the instruments. The string instruments look similar, but are different in size and sound. They all have strings, which are played with your fingers or a bow.

There are four families of instruments in an orchestra: [1] ____, [2] ____, [3] ____ and [4] ____ . The [5] ____ is the person who tells the [6] ____ when to play their instruments.

3 **Read again and answer the questions.**

1 Which is the loudest family of instruments?
2 Which is the largest family of instruments?
3 Which two families of instruments do musicians blow into?
4 Which family of instruments keep the rhythm of the music?
5 Which family of instruments do you play with a bow or your fingers?

4 **Match the beginnings and ends of the phrases.**

1 press   a a bow to play an instrument
2 use   b the holes of an instrument
3 blow   c into an instrument
4 cover and uncover   d the rhythm of the music
5 keep   e the keys on an instrument

5 **Copy and complete the table with the four instrument families.**

1 _____		
clarinet	oboe	flute
2 _____		
drum	cymbal	tambourine
3 _____		
trumpet	trombone	tuba
4 _____		
viola	violin	cello

6 🔊 **Listen to four different instruments. Say what family of instruments each one is from.**

7 **Discuss.**

● Which of the instruments that you heard today did you like best and why?
● If you could play one instrument in the orchestra, which would it be and why?

Project: your song

You are going to share your favourite song with the rest of the class.

1. Choose one song that means a lot to you. Find and print several copies of the words of the song. Check that you understand what all the words mean.

2. Prepare your answers to these questions.
   - What's the name of the song and who wrote or performed it?
   - Why is it important to you?
   - How does it make you feel?

3. Work in groups. Take it in turns to:
   - give copies of your song words to the rest of your group
   - help other students with any words that they don't understand in the song
   - play a part of the song for them (if possible)
   - talk about the song and explain why it's important to you and how it makes you feel
   - answer any questions about your choice of song.

4. When you listen to other students' songs, ask questions to find out as much as possible about their choice.

5. Compare the songs that you chose in your group. Were they similar or different? Did you choose songs for the same reasons? Did they make you feel the same way?

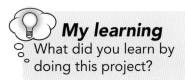

My learning
What did you learn by doing this project?

City life 10

Looking forward

This unit focuses on city life. You will consider whether it's better to live in a city or the country, think about what makes a great city, and design your own ideal city.

You will read
- about what makes a great city
- about the top five cities to live in

You will listen
- to a debate about whether it is better to live in a city or in the country

You will speak
- about the advantages and disadvantages of living in a city and in the country
- about your favourite city in a short presentation

You will write
- a description of your favourite city

You will learn
- to use reported commands
- to use the infinitive after adjectives and verbs
- to use noun phrases

City or country life?

1 **Discuss.**

- Do you live in a town or city or do you live in a village in the country?
- What are the advantages and disadvantages of living in a town or city?
- What are the advantages and disadvantages of living in the country?

2 **Who prefers to live in the city? Who prefers to live in the country? Take a class vote.**

3 (10A) **Listen once and choose the correct options.**

The topic of debate is whether it's ¹[better / worse] to live in the country than the city. Frank Hardy ²[agrees / disagrees] with this and Michael Vierra ³[agrees / disagrees].

4 (10A) **Read the *Listening tip* and listen again. Note down three expressions that Frank uses and three phrases that Michael uses.**

5 (10A) **Listen again and discuss.**

- What four points does Frank make to back up his argument?
- What four points does Michael make to back up his argument?
- Do you think their arguments are good? Why? / Why not?

6 **Take another class vote on the topic. Has anyone changed their minds after listening to the speakers' arguments?**

7 (10A) **Listen again to how these adjectives are used in sentences. Then match the adjectives to the correct definition.**

1	experienced	a	near or easy to get to
2	knowledgeable	b	in or related to the area you live in
3	local	c	with a lot of energy
4	peaceful	d	knowing a lot about a particular subject
5	convenient	e	knowing something because you've done it for a long time
6	lively	f	quiet and calm

Language tip

A *debate* is a long discussion or argument about a particular *topic* (subject) where two or more people give different opinions. At the end of a debate, people might take a *vote* to show which side of the argument they agree with.

Listening tip

When you are listening to someone explaining an argument, you may hear expressions that:

introduce their opinion: *As far as I'm concerned ... ; In my opinion, ... ; In my view, ...*

introduce the first point: *First, ... ; Firstly, ... ; To begin, ...*

break up the points: *What's more, ... ; Next, ... ; Also, ...*

finish the argument: *To finish, ... ; Finally, ... ; In conclusion, ...*

1 Copy and complete the commands from the debate with the words from the box.

Don't look down　　Put　　Look up　　Don't be　　Have　　Don't take

1 "____ your hands together for Frank, please!"　　2 "____ my word for it!"

3 "____ a look at house prices online!"　　4 "____ shy everyone!"

5 "____ at your feet!"　　6 "____ at the beautiful buildings around you!"

2 Look at the examples and match the sentences to complete the grammar rules.

*Jane **told** us **to put** our hands together for Frank.*

*Frank **asked** us **not to take** his word for it.*

1 To report a command,

2 To report a negative command,

3 The tenses of the verb

4 Pronouns and time phrases

a <u>don't change</u> in the way they do in reported statements and questions.

b use *tell / ask* + someone + *not to* + verb.

c use *tell / ask* + someone + *to* + verb.

d <u>change</u> in the same way they do in reported statements and questions.

3 Copy and complete the reported commands for sentences 3–6 from Activity 1.

1 Frank ____ look at house prices online.　　2 Jane ____ shy.

3 Michael ____ at our feet.　　4 Michael ____ the beautiful buildings around us.

1 (10B) Listen to these four exclamations about the debate. What intonation do the speakers use at the end? Choose the correct pattern.

rise and fall intonation　　rising intonation

What a ridiculous argument!　　*Nonsense!*

That's crazy!　　*I don't believe it!*

2 Repeat the exclamations in Activity 1. Then say the following exclamations with the same intonation.

Living in a city is exciting!

There's so much to do!

I love living here!

What makes a great city?

1 **Look and match the phrases and the photos.**

1 plenty of job opportunities
2 beautiful, original architecture
3 reliable transport system
4 interesting, friendly people
5 lively, exciting culture
6 parks and open spaces

a    b    c

d    e    f

2 **What do you think is important in a city? Rank the things in Activity 1 from *least important* to *most important*.**

☐   ☐   ☐   ☐   ☐   ☐

least important ———————————————→ most important

Reading: great cities of the world

1 **Read and match the sentences (1–5) with the spaces (a–e) at the start of each paragraph on the next page.**

1 A great city is a city that has space to breathe.
2 A great city is an exciting place to be!
3 A great city is only as great as the people who live there!
4 A great city is one that never stops moving.
5 A great city is a city at work.

2 **Which of the descriptions from *Vocabulary: a great city* is not mentioned in the article?**

> **Reading tip**
> The first sentence of each paragraph often gives you a summary of the whole paragraph. This can be useful if you have to read a text quickly.

What makes a great city?

A recent survey has shown what people are really looking for in their cities. You may be shocked to find out the results!

a ____ From great theatres, cafes and restaurants to interesting museums, art galleries and exhibitions, a lively culture appears to be important to a lot of people.

b ____ Cities continue to be expensive places to live, so there must be enough employment for all the people who live in them. In fact, many people move to cities because they think they are more likely to find interesting, new jobs there.

c ____ Parks and green spaces are very important to help people to escape from the stress of city living. Reports have shown that green spaces have important health benefits for people.

d ____ People living in cities often have to travel large distances to get to work, so they expect cities to have good trains, buses and taxis as well as great roads.

e ____ Cities can be lonely places, even though they are full of people, so a smile from a stranger is certain to make all the difference!

---

3 Read the *Reading tip*, then answer the questions.

1 Why are cities exciting places to live?

2 Why is it important for people living in cities to find jobs?

3 Why are green spaces important for people living in cities?

4 Why is transport important to people in cities?

5 Why are friendly people important in cities?

Reading tip

When you are reading an article, ask yourself *why* questions to check that you've understood the writer's reasons.

4 Discuss.

● Do you think that the place where you live is great? Why? / Why not?

● Does it have the things mentioned in the article?

Vocabulary: words in context

Find nouns in the article for these definitions.

1 a place where people go to look at art

2 a public event where art or interesting objects are shown

3 an unpleasant feeling of worry caused by difficulties in life

4 a thing that helps you or gives you an advantage

5 the amount of space between two places

6 a person you don't know

Use of English: infinitive after adjectives and verbs

1 Copy and complete the sentences from the article with *to* and a verb from the box. Then look back at the article to check your answers.

> be   find   have   hear   make

1   You may be **shocked** ____ the results!

2   Many people move to cities because they think they are more **likely** ____ interesting, new jobs there.

3   A smile from a stranger is **certain** ____ all the difference!

4   A lively culture **appears** ____ important to a lot of people.

5   Residents **expect** ____ good trains, buses and taxis as well as great roads.

2 Make new sentences using the adjectives and verbs in brackets.

1   This shop looks as if it is open. (appears)

> *The shop appears to be open.*

2   The train will definitely be on time. (certain)

3   I was surprised to see Josh in the city. (shocked)

4   Kim will probably get the job. (likely)

5   Olivia believes she will move house next week. (expects)

6   This restaurant carries on producing delicious food. (continue)

Use of English: noun phrases

1 Read the *Language tip*, then find five noun phrases in the article on page 113.

2 Make these sentences more interesting by adding noun phrases.

1   The teacher visited an exhibition.

> My lovely, kind history teacher visited an exciting, new exhibition about the history of our great city!

2   Jan got a job.

3   Reema went by train.

4   Sam had lunch in the park.

5   The children are at the museum.

Speaking: giving a short presentation about *My favourite city*

1 Read the *Speaking tip* and plan your presentation by answering these questions in note form. Look again at the *Listening tip* on page 110 for examples of phrases that you could use in your presentation.

- What's the best city you've ever been to and what country is it in?
- Thinking about this city, what can you say about the following?

  people   architecture   culture   transport

  parks and open spaces   job opportunities

- Why do you like this city so much?

2 Work in groups. Give your presentations and listen to other students. Ask questions at the end of other students' presentations.

Speaking tip

Don't feel nervous about giving a presentation. It's just talking!

Plan your presentation with an introduction, a few key points and a conclusion.

Use details and examples to support the main points of your presentation.

Speak slowly and clearly in formal English.

Use visual aids if you think they will be useful.

My learning

What parts of your presentation do you think were most successful? What will you do differently next time?

Writing: a description of your favourite city

1 Read the *Writing tip*. Match the adjectives on the left with the more interesting alternatives on the right.

1	very old	a	huge
2	nice	b	inexpensive
3	big	c	tiny
4	busy	d	ancient
5	cheap	e	lively
6	small	f	charming

Writing tip

Use complex noun phrases to make your writing more interesting. For example, don't use <u>boring adjectives</u>! Use <u>exciting, colourful and interesting adjectives</u>!

2 Write a description of your favourite city, using the notes you made for your presentation as your plan. Use some of the interesting adjectives in Activity 1 and look in your dictionary to find more.

Read your work and ask yourself the following questions:

- Have I used the *Listening tips* from page 110 correctly?
- Have I used adjectives correctly?
- Have I used any noun phrases?
- Have I checked my spelling?
- Have I checked my grammar?

Focus on the World

The best cities in the world

1 What do you think the phrase *quality of life* means? What things do you think are important for a person's *quality of life*?

2 Read <u>just</u> the introduction to the article. Which cities do you think will be in the top five?

> A recent report has studied the quality of life in 450 cities across the world. The researchers looked at a number of different things, including politics, economics, social freedom, health centres, education, transport, culture, shops, houses and the natural environment. From this, they made a list of the best cities in the world to live. Here are the top five!

3 Read the rest of the article, look at the photos and match to the correct cities.

1  2  3

4  5

A   Vienna, Austria

Population	1 741 246
Size	415 km²

- Sometimes called the City of Music because more famous musicians have lived here than in any other city.

- Home to the world's oldest big wheel, The Weiner Riesenrad, which is very famous and appeared in the 1949 film *The Third Man*.

B   Zurich, Switzerland

Population	391 359
Size	88 km²

- Millions come to the city every August for Street Parade – the largest street party in Europe.

- Home to over 1200 drinking fountains, you won't get thirsty here!

C   Auckland, New Zealand

Population	1 415 550
Size	1086 km²

- There are around 50 volcanoes in and around Auckland.

- Its nickname is City of Sails because one in three people who live in Auckland have boats.

D   Munich, Germany

Population	1 407 835
Size	311 km²

- The largest museum of science and technology in the world is here – Deutsches Museum displays more than 28 000 objects and has 1.5 million visitors every year.

- The Olympic Games of 1972 were important for Munich – the underground was built for the Games, and cars were no longer allowed on the streets of the old town, only pedestrians.

E   Vancouver, Canada

Population	603 502
Size	115 km²

- Greenpeace was started here in 1971, after a group of volunteers met in a café.

- Home to Canada's longest pool – this outdoor, saltwater pool is 137.5 metres long, which is nearly the size of three Olympic pools.

4   Read again and answer the questions.

1   Which city has the most square metres?
2   Which city is known as the City of Sails?
3   Which city has the biggest population?
4   Which city hosted the Olympic Games in 1972?
5   Which city has a long swimming pool?
6   Which city has a lot of water fountains?

5   Match the words from the first paragraph of the article to the correct definition.

1   politics
2   economics
3   social freedom
4   health centres
5   education

a   places for treating illnesses and injuries
b   being able to do what you want in society
c   teaching and learning
d   activities and ideas concerned with government
e   the way in which money is organised in society

6   Research one more interesting fact about each of the cities in the article.

7   Discuss.

- Have you been to any of the cities mentioned in the article?
- Which would you most like to visit and why?
- What are your top five cities of the world and why?

Project: design an ideal city

You are going to work in groups to design a new, ideal city. You will present this information on a poster.

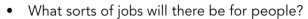

1 Brainstorm ideas for your city.

- Where will your city be? How big will it be? How many people will live there?

- What types of transport will you use? Will you consider not allowing cars in your city?

- What sorts of jobs will there be for people?

- What percentage of your city will be parks and open spaces?

- What sorts of houses will people live in?

- What sorts of culture will there be in your city?

- Will it be a green city? Will people use green energy?

- Think of a name for your city.

2 Research information for your city.

- Divide the questions in Activity 1 up between members of your group and write notes about each question for your poster and presentation.

- Draw or find pictures of the sorts of architecture you would like to have in your city.

- Sketch a rough map of your city centre showing where all the places you want will be.

3 Design your poster. Use the material you have gathered. Make the poster as interesting and attractive as possible.

4 Prepare and give a presentation. Work together to talk about the choices you have made about your ideal city. Answer any follow-up questions.

5 Share your thoughts.

- Listen to other presentations and ask questions.

- Did you have similar ideas or were they all different?

- Which group came up with the most unusual idea for their city?

- Which group thought of the most interesting name for their city?

My learning
What did you learn by doing this project?

Review 4

Speaking: talking about news stories

Discuss in pairs.

1   Look at these photos. What is the story of each picture?

2   Look at the photos below and write down six reasons why a city can be great.

3   Read the news stories again (pages 100 and 113) to check your answers.

Listening: city or country?

1   Read these two parts of the debate from Unit 10. Write down the correct words to complete the paragraphs.

Firstly, the air is cleaner in the country than it is in the city. We don't have nearly as much pollution here. What's more, it's ^{1}___ to live in the country than in the city. Don't take my word for it! Have a look at house prices online! Also, people who live in the country feel like they are part of a ^{2}___ community. They say the loneliest places in the world are big cities and I can believe that. To finish, it's ^{3}___ and quiet in the country. That's why I love living there!

To begin, it's very ^{4}___ because we have the whole world on our doorstep. When I want to get my hair done, there's a hairdresser five minutes from my flat. If I want to have my car washed, there's a garage just two minutes away. Next, my city is so ^{5}___ and exciting! Every weekend I do something different. From museums to shops, theatres to sports centres, I almost have too much choice! Also, we get to look at amazing buildings every day. Next time you walk through a city, don't look down at your feet! Look up at the beautiful buildings around you. Finally, we get to meet all sorts of ^{6}___ people. I'm always learning because I meet interesting new people all the time! That's why I love living in a city!

2   Now listen and check your answers. How many did you get right?

Writing: a blog post

Write a blog post on this subject: *Would you rather live in a big city, a small town or the countryside?* **Look again at page 105 to see how to plan your blog post.**

Vocabulary: music and cities

Can you name:

- three ways that music can change the world?
- three adjectives to describe feelings?
- five adjectives to describe cities?
- five places in cities?
- five things you think are important in a great city?

Use of English: relative clauses

Work in pairs. Think of an object, a person, a place and a time of year. Describe them without saying the word. Can your partner guess the words?

This is a time of year when it's cold and sometimes it snows. (winter)

Use of English: reported questions and commands

1 **Work in pairs, Student A and Student B. Rewrite the direct questions and commands in your box in reported speech.**

> **Student A:**
>
> 1 "Did you visit London?" Flora asked Lee.
> 2 Jon asked Lucy, "What are you doing?"
> 3 "Did you stay in an apartment or a hotel?" Francois asked Pieter.
> 4 "Don't listen to this song!" Stevan told his brother.
> 5 The teacher told the children, "Play your instruments loudly!"
> 6 "Close the door!" Kim told Natalia.

> **Student B:**
>
> 1 "What song did you buy?" Simone asked Samira.
> 2 "Have you ever been to Paris?" Richard asked Tom.
> 3 Franco asked Isabel, "Are you going to study music or architecture?"
> 4 "Turn the music down!" Sarah told her son.
> 5 Ayesha told Anna, "Pass me the book!"
> 6 "Don't forget your lunch!" Janet told Emily.

2 **Swap notebooks. Read and correct each other's sentences.**

3 **Check your answers with the teacher. You get one point for each correct sentence. The pair with the most points is the winner.**

A job for life

11

Looking forward

This unit focuses on the world of work and what is a good job. You will have the opportunity to think about what job you would like to do.

You will read
- an article about jobs that make people happy
- about analysing data in Maths

You will listen
- to a student podcast about jobs

You will speak
- about what you are looking for in a job

You will write
- a description of your dream job

You will learn
- to use phrasal verbs with *put*
- to ask questions politely
- to use modal verbs

The happiest jobs

1 These are the five most enjoyable jobs in the world, according to a recent questionnaire. What order do you think they came in? Rank them 1–5.

nurse   gardener   engineer   teacher   doctor

2 Read and match them with the jobs in the box in Activity 1. Are you surprised by the most enjoyable job? Why? / Why not?

The happiest jobs in the world

A recent questionnaire has produced a list of the most enjoyable jobs in the world. Engineers came first, followed by teachers and nurses. Interestingly, there was no link between earning a lot of money and being happy in your job. We spoke to some workers in the top five jobs to find out why their work makes them so happy.

1 __

"It feels great when I see my designs become something real! I don't mind the long hours because my job doesn't feel like work at all. It's very similar to my hobbies, in fact!"

2 __

"I love working with kids! They are funny, intelligent and usually want to make the world a better place. I love seeing their smiling faces as they put their hands up! Also, there's a lot of variety every day – I never get bored!"

3 __

"Every day, I make a difference – every day, I go home knowing that I've helped a sick child and their family. Sometimes, I get to know people really well and see children grow up too."

4 __

"I enjoy meeting my patients and having the opportunity to improve their quality of life. Also, I enjoy being part of a team, working with other doctors and with nurses. Sometimes, I travel abroad to do operations in different countries, which is always interesting."

5 __

"I love working outdoors in the fresh air – I get to work with nature and enjoy the changing seasons. I also love seeing how gardening or a lovely garden can bring such happiness to people."

3 Read again and match.

1 The engineer enjoys his / her job because ...

2 The teacher enjoys his / her job because …

3 The nurse enjoys his / her job because …

4 The doctor enjoys his / her job because …

5 The gardener enjoys his / her job because …

a he / she builds strong relationships with the people they care for.

b he / she gets to work in different countries.

c he / she gets to make people happy with their work.

d he / she does a lot of different things every day.

e his / her work is similar to their hobbies.

Vocabulary: multi-word verbs with *put*

1 Read the *Language tip* and complete the sentence from the article.

I love seeing their smiling faces as they ___ their hands ___.

2 Read more examples of multi-word verbs with *put* and match them to the correct definitions.

1 *Please wait while I **put** you **through**.*

2 *Can you **put** that book **away**, please.*

3 *She **put** the bags **down** while she waited.*

4 *I don't want to **put** the TV **on** at the moment.*

5 *The pan caught fire, so I **put** it **out**.*

6 *Can we **put** our meeting **off** until tomorrow?*

a stop holding something and place it on a surface

b make a piece of electrical equipment start working

c connect someone on the telephone to the person they want to speak to

d delay doing something

e put something back in the place where it is usually kept

f make a fire stop

> **Language tip**
>
> Some verbs are made up of two words, a verb and a preposition, for example:
>
> *He **took** his coat **off**.*
>
> We call these multi-word verbs.

3 Make your own sentences with three of the multi-word verbs with *put* from Activity 2.

My dream job

1 **Read and match the jobs to the descriptions.**

designer   scientist   vet   musician   firefighter   lawyer

Why do you love your job?

1 I love taking care of animals and making them better.

2 My job makes the world a safer place because I help to put criminals into prison.

3 My job is very creative because I always have to come up with new styles and ideas.

4 My job is important because we do experiments that really make a difference to medicine.

5 I get paid to do the thing I love most and I make people happy with my music at the same time!

6 Although my job can be dangerous, it's very important and sometimes we save people's lives.

2 **Discuss.**

- Which of the jobs in Activity 1 would you most like to do and why?
- Which would you least like to do and why?
- What's your dream job and why?

Speaking tip

Make your spoken English more interesting by including details and examples to illustrate your main points.

Listening: I want to be a …

1 **(11)** **What jobs do the students want to do? Listen and choose the correct options.**

1 Jared

a

b

c

2 Claudia

 a
 b
 c

3 Rob

 a
 b
 c

2 🔊 11 **Listen again and answer the questions.**

1 Why does Dina tell Jared that he should get a part-time job?

2 What job does Jared's uncle do?

3 What jobs do Claudia's parents do?

4 Why does Claudia need to learn French?

5 Why has Rob now decided against the jobs he wanted to do when he was younger?

6 Why does Rob want to be a lawyer?

Vocabulary: talking about jobs

Read the sentences from the podcast and match the words in italics to the correct definition.

1 It will mean years of *training*, so I may not be able to afford it.

2 You should get a *part-time job* and start saving money now.

3 I'm not sure what *career* I want yet.

4 I did some *work experience* last summer and I really enjoyed it.

5 I want a job with a good *salary*!

a a job where you only work for part of each day or week

b learning the skills you need to do a job

c the money you earn from your job

d when you do a job for a short period of time (usually when you're a student) to see if you enjoy it

e the type of work you want to do for all your working life

Use of English: asking questions politely

1 Complete the questions from the recording with words from the box.

> do   wonder   could

1 I ___ if you could tell me what you want to be when you grow up?
2 ___ you know what you want to be when you grow up?
3 ___ you tell me what you want to be when you grow up?

2 Say this direct question in the correct order.

be / grow up? / you / when / What / you / do / to / want

3 Choose the correct options to complete the rules.

1 The questions in Activity 1 are [more / less] polite than the question in Activity 2.
2 The word order of polite questions is [the same as / different from] direct questions.
3 We [use / don't use] verbs *do*, *does* and *did* in polite questions.
4 We [use / don't use] *if / whether* when we are making yes / no questions more polite.

4 Ask your partner two polite questions.

Use of English: using modal verbs

1 Read the *Language tip* and find eight modal verbs in the sentences from the recording.

1 *Could you answer a question for my podcast?*
2 *I think I might become a vet.*
3 *I may not be able to afford it.*
4 *You should get a part-time job.*
5 *My uncle is a farmer, so I may work with him on the farm.*
6 *You shouldn't give up your dreams.*
7 *It might not be easy, but it's worth a try!*
8 *Would you answer a question for me quickly?*

> **Language tip**
>
> A modal verb is used before a main verb to give additional information, for example:
>
> *I've been talking to some students about what jobs they **might** do in the future.*

2 Look again at the examples in Activity 1 and match the modal verbs to their use.

1 *might, might not / may, may not*
2 *should, shouldn't*
3 *Would …, Could …*

a to make a suggestion / give advice
b to ask somebody to do something
c to talk about something that is possible

3 Write sentences with modal verbs.

- Make a suggestion / give advice about learning vocabulary.
- Ask your partner to give you their book.
- Say something that it's possible you will do this weekend.

indirect and embedded questions; modals of possibility, request and suggestion

Speaking: explaining your opinion

1 Read and discuss the sentences from the recording. Tell your partner if you agree or disagree.

> *I really want to do a job that helps people.*

> *I just want a job that I find interesting and that I enjoy.*

> *I want a job with a good salary!*

2 Rank these things in order from least important to most important when it comes to a job you want to do in the future. Discuss with a partner. Use the expressions from the *Language tip* to explain your opinions.

> helping people   interesting work
>
> good salary   good working hours
>
> good people to work with   chance to learn new things

least important ————————————————▶ *most important*

Language tip
Use these phrases to explain your opinion:

I feel this way because …

This is important to me because …

I believe this because …

The reason I've chosen this is that …

Writing: a description of your dream job

1 You're going to write an essay: *My dream job.* Answer the questions with notes to write a plan.

Paragraph one: What do you like about your dream job?

Paragraph two: What training do you need to do this job?

Paragraph three: How are you going to get your dream job?

2 Write your description but do not include the name of the job.

Read and edit your work. Check:

- Have I followed the essay outline in Activity 1?
- Have I incuded the name of the job by mistake?
- Have I checked my spelling?
- Have I checked my grammar?

3 Swap descriptions with a partner. Can you work out your partner's dream job?

Spelling tip
Note how *doctor* and *inventor* both end with *–or.* Other jobs that end in *–or* include *actor, author, editor, director, supervisor, solicitor* and *professor.*

Be careful because there are also a lot of jobs that end with *–er* and the sound is similar to the *–or* words, for example: *teacher, cleaner, firefighter, driver* and *plumber.*

Focus on Maths

Analysing data

1 Discuss.

- Have you ever asked or been asked questions for a survey? What was it about?
- Why do you think people do surveys? What do they use the information for?

2 Copy and complete the introduction to a survey.

data   survey   analyse

A ¹ _____ was carried out in an office recently. Look at
the ² _____ in the table and read about the ways we
can ³ _____ it.

3 Read the rest of the text and answer the questions.

1 What was this survey about?

2 How many people were asked questions?

3 How many different ways was this data analysed?

How long it takes people to travel to work (in minutes)							
Sean	10	Chen	10	Tom	60
Lucinda	85	Kiera	10	Neema	50
Richard	20	Adanya	5	Laurence	20

MEAN

To **calculate** the **mean**, **add** the numbers together and **divide** by the number
of things / people.

$(10 + 85 + 20 + 10 + 10 + 5 + 60 + 50 + 20) \div 9 = 30$

mean = <u>30 minutes</u>

MEDIAN

To find the **median**, put all the numbers in order. The middle number is the
median number.

5   10   10   10   **20**   20   50   60   85

median = <u>20 minutes</u>

read non-fiction texts; understand detail in a technical text

MODE

The **mode** is the value that occurs most often. It's useful to put the numbers in order when you try to find the mode.

5   **10**   **10**   **10**   20   20   50   60   85

mode = <u>10 minutes</u>

RANGE

The **range** is the difference between the highest and lowest numbers in a set of numbers. To calculate the range, **subtract** the smallest number from the biggest number.

85 – 5 = 80

range = <u>80 minutes</u>

4 Find bold words in the text that mean:

1 find out an amount using numbers

2 take one number away from another number

3 the amount you get if you add a set of numbers together and divide them by the number of items in the set

4 the number that appears the most often in a set

5 the difference between the biggest and smallest number in a set of numbers

6 the number that is in the middle of a set of numbers

7 to calculate the total of two or more numbers

8 find out how many times one number can fit into another bigger number

5 Analyse the data in the table below to calculate the following information. Show how you work out each answer.

1 the mean

2 the median

3 the mode

4 the range

How many hours people work each week (in hours)					
Sean	40	Chen	10	Tom	10
Lucinda	15	Kiera	35	Neema	15
Richard	25	Adanya	15	Laurence	15

6 Work in pairs. Take it in turns to say the name of one of the methods of analysing data that you have used today and explain how you calculate it.

Project: a survey about jobs

You are going to do a survey about jobs and think about the results.

1 Copy the table below for your survey and think about how you will answer the question. How do you think other people might answer the question?

What's the most important thing you will look for in a future job?	tally	total
helping people		
interesting work		
good salary		
good working hours		
good people to work with		
chance to learn new things		

2 Carry out your survey, talking to as many people as possible. Remember to use polite questions and to complete your table.

I wonder if you could tell me …

Could you tell me …

I wonder if I could ask you …

Do you know …

> **Language tip**
> A *tally* is a way of keeping count during a survey.
>
> one = I   two = I I
>
> three = I I I   four = I I I I
>
> five = ⊬⊬

3 Think about your survey results. What do you think you can learn from them? Write sentences to describe your results and your conclusions.

Most students think that …

Not many students think that …

… is more important than … to most students.

4 Share your results with a partner. Do you have the same results and have you made the same conclusions about the results? Do you think you asked enough people to make your results reliable?

 **My learning**
What did you learn by doing this project?

Helping hand

12

Looking forward

This unit considers charities and the work they do, and also focuses on the importance of kindness.

You will read
- an article about different charities
- an extract from a novel, *Wonder*, by RJ Palacio

You will listen
- to a podcast about helping people

You will speak
- about ways to help people
- about which charity you would like your school to support

You will write
- a letter to your head teacher to persuade them to support a charity

You will learn
- to use modal verbs
- to use pronouns such as *anywhere, someone, anybody*
- to use likely and unlikely conditionals

Happy to help

1 Read this Chinese proverb and choose the best description of what it means.

If you want happiness for an hour, have a little sleep. If you want happiness for a day, go fishing. If you want happiness for a year, get a lot of money. If you want happiness for a lifetime, help somebody.

a   Helping other people is the key to feeling happy yourself.

b   Sleep and money are most important for happiness.

c   When you help other people, it makes them happy.

2 Discuss.

- Do you agree or disagree with this proverb? Explain your answer.
- What have you done to help someone this week?
- How do you feel when you help someone?

3 (12A) Listen and choose the correct options.

1   A *suspended coffee* is a coffee you buy for [a friend / someone you don't know].

2   The two people who are interviewed agree that suspended coffees are a [good / bad] idea.

3   The presenter of the podcast wants us all to [start / stop] buying suspended coffees.

4 Discuss.

- Do you like the idea of buying a suspended coffee for someone? Why? / Why not?
- Will you start buying them in the future?

5 (12A) Listen again. Are the following sentences *True* or *False*? Correct any false sentences.

1   The people who take the suspended coffees have to pay for them.

2   The woman interviewed thinks that a suspended coffee is about showing that people still care.

3   The man interviewed buys suspended coffees because he wants to help someone straight away in his community.

4   If your local café doesn't sell suspended coffees, then you should give money to a local charity instead.

5   Buying a suspended coffee is a way of trying to get big charities to pay attention to local communities.

Vocabulary: words in context

1 Read the sentences from the podcast and match the words in bold to the correct definition.

1 *The money I spend isn't going to a big **charity**.*

2 *It's about showing people that people still **care**.*

3 *I think it's our **duty** as citizens.*

4 *Get your local café **involved**.*

5 *We must remember that **kindness** can be very simple.*

6 *Buying a coffee for a **stranger** is a way of trying to change the world.*

a taking part in something

b someone you've never met before

c something that you feel you have to do

d be interested in someone or something

e the act of being friendly and helpful

f an organisation that collects money for people who need help

Use of English: using modal verbs

1 Copy and complete the sentences from the podcast with the words from the box.

> mustn't forget   have to look after   don't have to prove
> must remember

1 *The people who take the coffees ___ that they need help.*

2 *We ___ that this is about more than just coffee.*

3 *We all ___ each other.*

4 *We ___ that kindness can be very simple.*

Language tip

We use the modal verbs *must* and *have to* to talk about what we need to do or to give strong advice. Take care though with the negatives, *mustn't* and *don't have to*, which have different meanings.

2 Match the sentences that have the same meaning.

1 *You **must / have to** go to school.*

2 *You **mustn't** go to school.*

3 *You **don't have to** go to school.*

a You aren't allowed to go to school.

b It isn't necessary to go to school, but you can if you want to.

c It is necessary to go to school. / I strongly suggest that you go to school.

3 Write sentences using the correct modal verbs from Activity 2.

● Something it is necessary for you to do every day.

● Something that it isn't necessary for you to do, but that you choose to do.

● Something that you're not allowed to do at school.

Which charity?

1 **Discuss.**

- Look at the photograph. What do you think the girl is doing? Have you ever volunteered to do something like this?
- Do you or your family support any charities? Which do you support and why?
- Does your school support any charities? What do you do to raise money?
- What other charities would you like to support?

2 **Read the report quickly and match the charity names (1–4) with the descriptions (a–d).**

1 Help the Arts
2 Fitness for Friends
3 Support the Environment
4 Look after Animals

Language tip

When you *support a charity*, you give your time or money to it.

When you *raise money*, you make money for a particular purpose, for example, a charity.

When you *volunteer*, you work without being paid because you want to do it.

Charities that we can support

a _____

This charity helps to deal with the problems facing our planet. It aims to:

- stop climate change around the world immediately
- protect forests by completely stopping people cutting down forests and by planting new trees
- look after the oceans and seas everywhere on our planet
- save the Arctic, which is disappearing quickly.

b _____

This charity helps to protect creatures from anybody who is cruel to them. This charity:

- improves the lives of animals on farms, in the wild, in laboratories and in homes.
- rescues animals that are in danger
- reports to the police people who are extremely cruel to animals
- finds new homes for animals that need them.

c _____

This charity helps people through art, music and drama. Their work includes:

- running art workshops to help people who can hardly speak to find a voice
- allowing people to deal with difficult experiences and find hope through drama
- bringing together a choir of people from different backgrounds and cultures
- organising exhibitions so that everybody can feel proud of their work.

d _____

This charity helps people in sport and uses sport to help people. The charity:

- supports future sports stars
- gives all children the opportunity to play sport
- helps disabled people who don't usually have access to sport
- uses sport to bring together divided communities.

3 Read Samira's thoughts about the report and find five things she says that are not true.

I've just read this report about the five charities we can support at school this year. The environmental charity looks interesting because it helps to protect forests, oceans and deserts. I like the idea of supporting the animal charity because it rescues and finds new homes for animals that are in danger. It doesn't help wild animals, though. The arts charity looks good, too. I like the fact that it helps people through drama and dance. If I have some free time next year, I'll join the choir. The sports charity also does important work. I think it's good that it provides sport for children, disabled people and elderly people, as well. If I had a lot of money, I would give some to all these charities!

> Samira says that there are five charities in the report, but there are only four.

Vocabulary: words in context

Match the words from the report to the correct definition.

1	protect	a	separated into smaller parts
2	cruel	b	deliberately making people suffer, unkind
3	rescue	c	ability to enter and use something
4	divided	d	save someone from a dangerous situation
5	disabled	e	keep someone or something safe
6	access	f	having an injury or condition that makes it difficult for you to work or live normally

Punctuation tip

Look at the lists in the report, which are broken up with bullet points. You can see that:

- each list is introduced with a sentence stem and a colon (:)
- each bullet point makes a different point
- each bullet point completes the sentence stem to make a full sentence
- the final bullet point has a full stop at the end.

Use of English: pronouns *somebody, nothing, anyone, etc ...*

1 Read the *Language tip* and look at these sentences from the report then answer the questions.

*This charity helps to protect creatures from **anybody** who is cruel to them.*

*Their work includes organising exhibitions so **everybody** feels proud of their work.*

1 Do we know who is cruel to animals?
2 Do we know who shows their work at the exhibitions?
3 Do we use the singular or plural verb after these types of pronouns?

Language tip

We sometimes use pronouns to talk about people or things when we don't know exactly who or what they are, for example, *anybody, no one, something, everything.*

2 Copy and complete the sentences with your own ideas.

- I think that everybody should …
- Last week, I met somebody who …
- Do you know anyone who …
- There is no one who …

Use of English: likely and unlikely conditionals

1 **Look at Samira's sentences.**

a *If I **have** some free time next year, I'**ll join** the choir.*

b *If I **won** a lot of money, I **would give** some to all the charities!*

   1   Which sentence talks about something that is likely to happen?

   2   Which sentence talks about something that is unlikely to happen?

2 **Look at the structure of the sentences.**

   1   Which sentence has a present simple tense in the first part of the sentence and *will* + verb in the second part of the sentence?

   2   Which sentence has a past simple tense in the first part of the sentence and *would* + verb in the second part of the sentence?

3 **Imagine that it's likely that you will have some free time next year. How will you help the charities?**

   If I have some free time next year, I'll …

4 **It's not very likely, but imagine that you won a lot of money. What would you do to help the charities?**

   If I won a lot of money, I'd…

5 ***What would happen?* Play a game.**

Work in groups. One person says a sentence. The next person makes a sentence using the second part of the previous sentence and adding their own idea.

> If I had lots of money, I'd buy my family a new house.

> If I bought my family a new house, we'd have a swimming pool.

> If we had a swimming pool, …

Speaking: discussing which charity to support

1 **Your school has raised £500 for charity. Choose to support a charity from the report on page 134.**

2 **Prepare your presentation.**

- Read again about your chosen charity and note down any important points.

- Think of arguments in favour of supporting your charity.

- What arguments do you think people might have against your charity? Decide how you could respond to these.

Language tip

When you have a discussion, you give arguments *in favour of* something (when you think it's a good thing) or *against* something (when you think it's a bad thing).

When you *persuade* someone, you make them agree with you by talking to them.

first and second conditionals; likely and unlikely conditionals; extended talk

3 **Match the useful expressions to their uses.**

1 Personally, I believe …
2 I see what you mean, but …
3 It's important to remember that …
4 But surely you can see that …

a to introduce an important point
b to disagree with something someone has said
c to give your opinion
d to try to persuade someone to see your point of view

4 **Work in small groups.**

- Use your notes from Activity 2 to give a short presentation about your charity.
- Listen to other presentations and discuss, using the expressions from Activity 3.
- Can your group agree on one charity to support? If not, then take a vote at the end.

5 **Talk to the rest of the class about your decisions. Do you all agree?**

Writing: a letter

1 **You're going to write a letter to your head teacher to persuade them to support your chosen charity. Complete the plan.**

Paragraph 1: Introduction – give your opinion	*In my opinion, …*
Paragraph 2: Argument 1 + reasons or examples	*First, …*
Paragraph 3: Argument 2 + reasons or examples	*In addition, …*
Paragraph 4: Argument 3 + reasons or examples	*What is more, …*
Paragraph 5: Conclusion – say your opinion again	*In conclusion, I believe that …*

2 **Write your letter.**

- Remember to start and finish the letter in the correct way.
- Use the useful expressions from the plan.

3 **Read and edit your letter.**

Focus on Literature

What's the author's message?

1 🔊 (12B) **Read and listen to the text and discuss the questions in the OVER TO YOU boxes.**

A   *Wonder*, by RJ Palacio, is about a ten-year old boy, August, who is about to start school for the first time. Read this extract from the first chapter.

August

I know I'm no ordinary ten-year-old kid. I mean, sure I do ordinary things. I eat ice cream. I ride my bike. I play ball. Stuff like that makes me ordinary. I guess. And I feel ordinary. Inside. But I know ordinary kids don't make other ordinary kids run away screaming in playgrounds. I know ordinary kids don't get looked at wherever they go… My name is August, by the way. I won't describe what I look like. Whatever you're thinking, it's probably worse.

Next week I start fifth grade. Since I've never been to a real school before, I am totally and completely terrified.

OVER TO YOU

1   How is August similar to other children and how is he different?

2   How do you think it feels to start a new school?

3   How does August feel about it? Why do you think he feels this way?

4   How would you feel if you were him?

5   What do you think will happen when August starts his new school?

B   Starting school is difficult for August. Some children are unkind to him because of the way he looks. But some children are kind. This extract is told by a girl called Summer.

Summer

I sat with him that first day because I felt sorry for him. That's all. Here he was, this strange-looking kid in a new school. No one was talking to him. Everyone was looking at him. All the girls at my table were talking about him. … And August knew it. It's hard enough being the new kid even when you have a normal face. Imagine having his face?

So I just went over and sat with him. Not a big thing. He's just a kid. The weirdest-looking kid I've ever seen, yes. But just a kid.

---

1 Why do you think some children were unkind to August?

2 How do you think August feels?

3 What would you do if August joined your school and you saw him sitting alone at lunchtime?

C   During the school year, August has some difficult times and is brave. At the end of the year, August's headmaster, Mr Tushman, is giving out prizes.

"The final prize this morning," said Mr Tushman, "is the Henry Ward Beecher medal for students who have done really well through the school year.

"While reading about Henry Ward's life, I found something that he wrote. Not just about kindness, but about our kindness. The power of our friendship. The test of our character. The strength of our courage. Courage. Kindness. Friendship. Character. These are the qualities that make us human and sometimes make us great. And this is what the Henry Ward Beecher medal is about: recognizing greatness.

"But how do we do that? How do we decide something like greatness? What does it even mean? Well, Beecher actually had an answer for that."

He put his reading glasses on again and started to read. " 'Greatness,' wrote Beecher, 'is not about being strong, but about using strength in the right way. He is the greatest whose strength carries up the most hearts…' This year I am very proud to give the Henry Ward Beecher medal to the student whose quiet strength has carried up the most hearts. So will August Pullman please come up here to receive this prize."…

I laughed and shook my head like I couldn't believe it. I really couldn't believe it. I think I was smiling. As I walked towards the stage, all I saw was happy, bright faces looking at me and hands clapping for me. …

I wasn't even sure why I was getting this medal, really.

No, that's not true. I knew why.

It's like people you see sometimes, and you can't imagine what it would be like to be that person, whether it's somebody in a wheelchair or somebody who can't talk. Only, I know that I'm that person to other people, maybe to every single person in that whole room.

To me, though, I'm just me. An ordinary kid.

But hey, if they want to give me a medal for being me, that's okay. I'll take it. I did just get through the fifth grade. And that's not easy, even if you're not me.

1 What award does August win and why?

2 Do you agree with Mr Tushman's definition of greatness? Why? / Why not?

3 How do you think August feels at the end?

2 Write definitions for these nouns used in the text. Use a dictionary to check meanings if you're not sure.

friendship   strength   courage   character   greatness

3 Discuss.
   ● What did you enjoy / not enjoy about reading parts of *Wonder*?
   ● What message do you think the author is trying to give readers in this book?

Project: the kindness project

If every person in this room made it a rule that wherever you are, whenever you can, you will try to act a little kinder than is necessary – the world really would be a better place.
From *Wonder* by RJ Palacio

You are going to work in groups to make posters and do a presentation about how you can make the world a better place by being kinder.

1 In small groups, discuss ways that you can encourage people to be kind at school. Use the ideas in the box or think of your own.

> notice and reward kindness   kindness wall or box for photos / messsages
>
> share kind photos / stories on social media   special courses in kindness
>
> kindness student reps   make a film about kindness   kindness posters
>
> kindness garden   kindness assemblies

2 Discuss some kind things you can do today. Use the ideas in the box or think of your own.

> say something nice to someone   help someone carry something
>
> let someone go ahead of you in a queue   write someone a letter
>
> pass on a book you've finished   pick up some rubbish   include people in conversations
>
> talk to someone you know is lonely   give up your seat on the bus
>
> listen when someone talks

3 Make a poster. Include your three best ideas:

- for making your school a kinder place.

- for kind things you can do today.

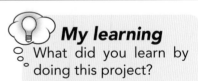

My learning
What did you learn by doing this project?

4 Prepare and give a presentation. Take turns to talk about your different ideas.

5 Look at the other posters, listen to presentations and ask questions. Who thought of the most original ideas?

6 Choose three ideas for kind things you can do and do them this week. Tell the class next week.

Review 5

Study tip
It's time to look back at what we have studied again. It helps us to learn.

Speaking: looking back

Work in pairs. Look back through Units 11 and 12. Find a picture of:

1 a job that you would like to do and explain why
2 a job that you wouldn't like to do and explain why
3 a charity that you would like to support and explain why.

Reading: a quiz

1 **Work in pairs. Find the answers to these questions in Units 11 and 12.**

  1 According to a recent article, what job is the most enjoyable in the world?
  2 When do we use a bullet point?
  3 According to a Chinese proverb, what should you do to be happy for a lifetime?
  4 What is a *suspended coffee* and would you ever buy one?
  5 What are the names of the charities that needed support in Unit 12?

2 **Write six more questions to ask about Units 11 and 12.**

3 **Work with another pair. Ask and answer their questions.**

Listening: choose the correct word

1 **These are two parts from the podcast about coffee and kindness. Choose the correct answers.**

It's about doing something for someone you ¹[know / don't know] and making their day a bit ²[better / worse].

We mustn't forget that this is about more than just coffee – it's about showing people that people still ³[care / don't care].

I like the fact that when I buy a suspended coffee for someone, the money I spend isn't going to a ⁴[big / small] charity – it's helping someone immediately in my ⁵[local / national] community. We all have to look ⁶[before / after] each other.

2 (12A) **Now listen and check your answers.**

Writing: a letter

1 **Write a letter to your teacher telling them what sort of job you would like to do in the future and why. Remember to start and finish the letter in the correct way.**

2 **Read and edit your letter. Check:**

  • Have you given clear reasons?
  • Have you started and finished the letter correctly?
  • Have you checked your spelling and grammar?

Vocabulary: talking about jobs

1 **What do these people do in their jobs?**

| designer | scientist | vet | musician | firefighter | lawyer |

2 **Copy and complete the text with the words from the box.**

| training | part-time | career | work experience | salary |

In the future, I want to have a ¹ ___ as an engineer, so I'm going to do some ² ___ next week at a local company to see if I like the work. If I do decide to study engineering, I will have to get a ³ ___ job. Then I will be able to use my ⁴ ___ to pay for my ⁵ ___ .

Use of English: asking questions politely

Work in pairs. Make these questions more polite. Then ask and answer them.

1 What job do you want to do when you grow up?
2 What three jobs do you think are the most important in the world?
3 What local charity would you like your school to support?
4 Do you think that buying a suspended coffee is a good way of helping others?
5 Will you ever buy someone a suspended coffee?

Use of English: multi-word and modal verb game

Work in pairs. Follow the instructions to play multi-word and modal verb noughts and crosses.

- Write your name on five small pieces of paper.
- Take it in turns to choose a square in the table. Make a sentence using the multi-word verb or modal verb in the square. If you both agree it is correct, put one of your papers on the square. If you don't agree that it is correct, ask your teacher to decide.
- The winner is the first to get three papers in a straight line (top to bottom, side to side or corner to corner).

might not	could	put through
don't have to	put down	may
put off	mustn't	shouldn't

should	put on	must
put out	may not	might
have to	would	put off

The digital generation

13

Looking forward

This unit focuses on the technology of today and how social media can become addictive. You will have the opportunity to consider how safe you are when you go online.

You will read
- a blog post about someone's relationship with their mobile phone
- about staying safe online

You will listen
- to a conversation about being addicted to technological devices

You will speak
- about how you use technological devices
- about the advantages and disadvantages of growing up in the digital age

You will write
- an essay about the advantages and disadvantages of growing up in the digital age

You will learn
- to talk about regrets
- to use abstract nouns
- to use multi-word verbs with *give*

Are you an addict?

1. Look at the picture and name the technological devices (equipment) you can see.

Language tip

If you are *addicted* to something you are unable to stop doing something that is harmful to you. The person who is addicted to something is called an *addict* and we say that they have an *addiction*.

2. Copy the arrow and rank the devices in Activity 1 from the one you *use least often* to the one you *use most often*.

→

use least often   *use most often*

3. Discuss.

- How much time do you spend on each of these devices every week?
- How much time do you spend on devices in total each week?
- How much time do you think is too much time? Why?
- Have you ever seen a situation like the picture in Activity 1 where everyone in a group of friends is on a different device and nobody is talking to each other? Do you think this is a good or bad thing? Why? / Why not?
- Do you think that you might be addicted to any of these devices? Why? / Why not?
- Which of these devices do you think is most popular in your class? Guess, then take a class vote of your favourite device to find out the answer.

Reading: addicted to technology

1. Guess the meaning of the word *nomophobic*.

   a   a fear of not having access to the internet

   b   a fear of not having a mobile phone

   c   a fear of not having any friends on social media

2 **Read the text quickly and check your answer to *Activity 1*. Then choose the best title for the blog post.**

a The day I gave up my phone

b Are mobile phones dangerous?

c Am I addicted to my phone?

What's the first thing you did this morning when you woke up? The first thing I did was look at my phone. I just wanted to check all my friends' status **updates** on **Facebook**. (Oh. Lots of photos of a friend's party. I wish I was more popular!)

I also just had to have a quick look to see if anyone had replied to my latest **tweet**. (No, no replies. And no **retweets** either. I wish I hadn't put that photo on **Twitter** now. I should have put it on **Snapchat** instead.)

And I also had to check **Instagram** to see how many **likes** and **comments** there had been for the funny video of the cat in a hat that I **posted**. (Only three likes and no comments. Oh dear! I shouldn't have **uploaded** that video of the stupid cat. I should have **shared** the video of the funny monkey on **YouTube** instead.)

I had to check all this on my phone before I even got out of bed this morning. And this is what I do every morning and every night too. Yes, I admit it. I'm addicted to my smartphone. In fact, I would go as far as to say that I'm nomophobic – I have a fear of having no mobile phone.

It's not just me. A recent report of people aged between 18 and 33 found that they used their smartphones for an average of five hours a day and checked them 85 times a day! Dr Richard Graham, an expert in technology addiction, suggests that addicts like me should try to *give up* their phones for a few days. So, last Saturday I thought I'd give it a try. How hard could it be? Very hard, apparently! I lasted exactly 27 and a half minutes before I gave in and reached for my phone. I just had to check Facebook, Twitter and Instagram … If only I was stronger! I'll try again next weekend!

Sara, Dublin

Reading tip

A blog post will usually have a heading and sometimes there will be space at the bottom for readers to leave comments. Blog posts are usually not that long and can contain pictures as well as words. They can be both formal and informal. This blog post is very informal and sounds as if the blogger is having a conversation with the reader.

Punctuation tip

When we want to say that something belongs to one person, we use apostrophe + s.

When we want to say that something belongs to more than one person, we add an apostrophe after the s.

*Lots of photos of a **friend's** party.* (= the party of one friend)

*I just wanted to check all my **friends'** status updates on Facebook.* (= the status updates of more than one friend)

Vocabulary: social media

Look at the words in bold in the blog post. Answer the questions in pairs.

1 Find the names of five social media sites in the blog post. Discuss what you think people use them for.

2 Find eight words related to things you do on social media which can be used as verbs or nouns. Discuss their meanings with your partner.

Reading: thinking about what the writer really feels

Discuss in pairs.

1 How do you think Sara felt when she checked:

   a Facebook   b Twitter   c Instagram

2 Do you use any of the social media sites mentioned in the text? Do you ever feel the way Sara did when you use them? When you post something online, are you always hoping for comments, likes or shares? Why? / Why not?

3 Sara talks about her friends on social media sites. Do you think that having friends on social media is the same as having friends in real life? Why? / Why not?

> ### Language tip
> A *regret* is a feeling of sadness or disappointment caused by something that someone does or doesn't do. We use *if only / I wish that* and *should / shouldn't have* to talk about regrets.

Use of English: talking about regrets

1 Copy and complete these sentences from the blog post.

1 *I wish I ___ more popular.*

2 *I wish I ___ that photo on Twitter.*

3 *I ___ it on Snapchat instead.*

4 *I ___ that video of the stupid cat.*

5 *I ___ the video of the funny monkey on YouTube.*

6 *If only I ___ stronger!*

2 Look at the examples and choose the correct option to complete the sentences.

1 When we regret something, we feel [sad / happy] about a situation.

2 We use *I wish / If only* + past simple to talk about things we regret about the [present / past].

3 We use *should / shouldn't have* + past participle to talk about things we regret about the [present / past].

3 Write sentences to talk about things that you regret in the present and in the past.

I wish I had …	*I wish I hadn't …*
If only I had …	*If only I hadn't …*
I should have …	*I shouldn't have …*

deduce meaning from context in reading; if only / wish that and should / shouldn't have

Growing up in the digital age

1 (13A) **Listen and complete the sentence.**

Tom and his mum are talking about:

a   giving up using their devices for a while because they are both addicted to them

b   how much they use their devices and how social media can be used for good

c   a friend of Tom's who has been sending kind tweets.

2 (13A) **Listen again and write down** *true, false* **or** *doesn't say.*

The report mentioned in the conversation says that:

1   one out of every two teenagers thinks that they have an addiction to a device

2   69% of parents think their children are addicted to their devices

3   teenagers are usually addicted to their smartphones

4   one-third of parents and teenagers disagree about device use every day

5   56% of parents admit to checking their phones while driving

6   69% of teenagers check their devices once an hour.

3 (13A) **Read the** *Listening tip*, **then listen again and think about what Tom and his mother are communicating without actually saying the words in these sentences.**

1   Mum: *It says half of all teenagers are addicted to their devices. Any thoughts, Tom?*

   a   She is asking his opinion on the report

   b   She is saying that she thinks he is one of the people who are addicted to their device.

2   Mum: *It also says here one-third of parents and teenagers argue about using devices every day …*

   Tom: *Hmmmm, that sounds familiar …*

   a   He is saying that this sounds like a situation that he saw in a film.

   b   He is saying that they are among the one-third of parents and teenagers who argue about using devices.

3   Mum: *Maybe we should try giving up our phones for a day or two?*

   Tom: *I don't think I need to bother answering that question …*

   a   He is saying that he is definitely not going to give up his phone.

   b   He is saying that he's too tired to answer the question.

> ## Listening tip
> Sometimes a speaker will communicate something without actually saying the words. Listen for clues to help you to understand these messages. Compare:
>
> *You didn't lock the front door this morning, Marie.*
>
> *The front door was unlocked when I got home. You were the last to leave this morning, Marie. Any ideas?*

Vocabulary: abstract nouns

1 Read the *Language tip*. In the box, find six abstract nouns that you heard in the recording.

> paper   teenager   thought   phone   success
>
> danger   opportunity   staff   happiness   sadness

Language tip

Some nouns are things we can see, hear, touch, smell or feel, for example, *device, computer, student*. Some nouns are different because they are ideas, thoughts or feelings, for example, *love, anger, hope*. We call these abstract nouns.

2 Choose three of the abstract nouns from Activity 1 and make sentences with them.

Vocabulary: multi-word verbs

1 Complete the multi-verb words from the recording.

1 *Maybe we should try giving ___ our phones for a day or two?*

2 *Give ___ my phone, please.*

2 Match the sentences to the correct definition of the multi-word verbs in italics.

1 I *gave up* coffee for a month.	a agree to do something although you don't really want to do it
2 He *gave back* my laptop when he had finished his work.	b give one of a number of things to each person in a group of people
3 Mum finally *gave in* and let me get a smartphone.	c give some written work to a teacher
4 Have you *given in* your project yet?	d give something to someone without asking for any money to pay for it
5 They were *giving away* chocolate at the shopping centre!	e return something to the person it belongs to
6 He *gave out* the dictionaries to the class.	f stop doing something

3 (13B) Listen to the sentences in Activity 2. For these multi-word verbs, which part do we stress?

4 Choose three of the multi-verb words from Activity 2 and say them in sentences.

Speaking: checking what someone said

1 (13C) Complete the table with the correct informal expressions.

> What was that?   I don't get your point.

Use	Formal	Informal
If you understand the words, but not the point someone is making.	*Sorry, but I don't follow you. Could you explain, please?*	1 _____
If you didn't hear what someone said.	*I'm afraid I missed that. Please could you say it again, a bit louder?*	2 _____

2 (13C) Listen and repeat.

Speaking tip

If you think you have understood someone's opinion but you're not sure, repeat it back to them and ask them to confirm.

Speaking: expressing your opinion

1 Read the sentence from the recording, then make notes to answer the questions.

It's much more complicated to grow up in the digital age than it was for people growing up 30 years ago.

1 What are the advantages of growing up in the digital age?

2 What are the disadvantages of growing up in the digital age?

3 Do you agree or disagree with Tom's mum? Why?

> **Speaking tip**
> When you're giving your opinion, use phrases such as:
>
> *I believe that ...*
> *In my opinion, ..*
> *In my view, ...*

2 Work in groups. Discuss the questions from Activity 1.

Use the expressions from *Speaking: checking what someone said* if you miss something that someone says.

3 Take a class vote. What do most students in your class think about this subject?

Writing: growing up in the digital age

1 You're going to write an essay: *Consider the advantages and disadvantages of growing up in the digital age.* Use your notes from Activity 1 of *Speaking: expressing your opinion* to write a plan.

Introduction	Introduce and explain the question	*In this essay, I am going to …*
Paragraph one	What are the advantages of growing up in the digital age?	*On the one hand, …*
Paragraph two	What are the disadvantages of growing up in the digital age?	*On the other hand, …*
Conclusion	What's your opinion?	*As far as I'm concerned, …*

2 Write your essay. Use the expressions in the table above.

3 Read your essay and ask yourself the following questions.

- Have I got an introduction and conclusion?
- Have I included advantages and disadvantages in different paragraphs?
- Have I included good examples to support my arguments?

4 Swap essays with a partner and read. Say two things you like about your partner's essay.

Focus on ICT

Staying safe online

1 **Discuss.**

- Have you ever felt uncomfortable or unsafe online? Why?
- What things do you do to stay safe online?

2 **Read the article and match the headings (1–6) to the paragraphs (a–f).**

1 Dangerous emails

3 Cyberbullying

5 Pictures and videos

2 Personal information

4 Being responsible online

6 Knowing who you are talking to

Top tips for staying safe online

a ___

Not everyone is who they say they are, and you shouldn't believe everything that you read. Don't make friends with people you don't know, and never arrange to meet somebody in real life who you have only spoken to on the internet.

b ___

Many websites ask you for information about yourself (for example, address, email address or mobile number). But be careful, because people can use your personal information for identity theft – for example, they might pretend to be you and shop online using your money. Only put your personal information on websites that you trust.

c ___

Think about who might look at pictures or watch videos that you post. Embarrassing photos can stay on the internet for years and might stop you from getting a job in the future.

d ___

Spam emails usually try to get you to buy something or to click on a link that might cause a virus on your computer. Phishing emails try to get you to reveal information about yourself, for example your bank details. Only give your email address out to people you can trust, and set up your email system so that it sends these types of emails straight to your junk folder.

e ___

Bullying online is just as bad as bullying in real life. If it happens to you or to someone you know, then you must tell somebody who can stop it from happening.

f ___

Keep your privacy settings as high as possible, and never tell anyone your passwords. Respect other people's views, and behave online in the way you would behave in real life. If you see anything that makes you feel uncomfortable, unsafe or worried, then leave the website, and tell an adult you trust about it immediately.

3 Give advice to these people using information from the text.

1 I'm going to meet a friend in a café after school. I've only met them online, but they've told me what they will be wearing, so that I recognise them when I arrive. Do you think that's OK?

2 I've just joined this new chat website and they've asked me for lots of information about where I live and what school I go to. Do you think it's OK for me to tell them?

3 I've got a really embarrassing photo of myself from last weekend. My friends will think it's so funny! Shall I put it online for everyone to enjoy?

4 I keep getting loads of spam emails. What can I do?

5 Some people are being really unkind to a friend of mine and they're telling lies about them online. It's making my friend really unhappy. What should I do?

6 I've seen a website that has really upset me. What should I do?

4 Match the words from the article to the correct definition.

1	cyberbullying	a	emails trying to sell you something
2	spam emails	b	emails trying to find out your personal information
3	phishing	c	controls to say who can look at your personal information
4	personal information	d	when someone is unkind online
5	identity theft	e	a secret word that lets you use a computer
6	privacy settings	f	part of your email system where spam emails are sent
7	password	g	a program that enters and destroys computers
8	virus	h	your address, your age, your school, and so on
9	click on a link	i	press on an icon to get to another website
10	junk folder	j	stealing someone's personal information

5 Tell your partner what you have learned in today's lesson. How will you behave differently online in future?

Project: our digital footprint

You're going to work in groups to make a poster about how to make sure your digital footprint is positive.

Language tip

Your *digital footprint* is the record of everything you do online, for example, your social media activity, information you've put on websites or photos or videos you've uploaded.

1. **Research and brainstorm to answer the questions.**

   - Why do you think it's important to have a positive digital footprint? Do some research, discuss the points in the box or think of your own ideas.

     > university and college applications
     >
     > scholarships   sports   club memberships
     >
     > job applications   identity theft

   - What things can be positive or negative in a digital footprint? Do some research, discuss the points in the box or think of your own ideas.

     > photos and videos   status updates
     >
     > likes on social media
     >
     > retweets and shares   comments on social media

   - Do you think having no digital footprint could be negative too? Why? / Why not?

2. **Consider all your ideas and choose the best to put on a poster. Include:**

   - reasons why it's important to have a positive digital footprint

   - ways of keeping your digital footprint positive.

   You could design your poster in the shape of a footprint like this one.

3. **Prepare and give a presentation. Work together to talk about the choices you have made. Answer any follow-up questions.**

4. **Share with the rest of the class.**

   - Listen to other presentations and ask questions.

   - Did you have similar ideas or were they all different?

   - Which group came up with the most useful way of keeping your digital footprint positive?

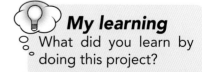
My learning
What did you learn by doing this project?

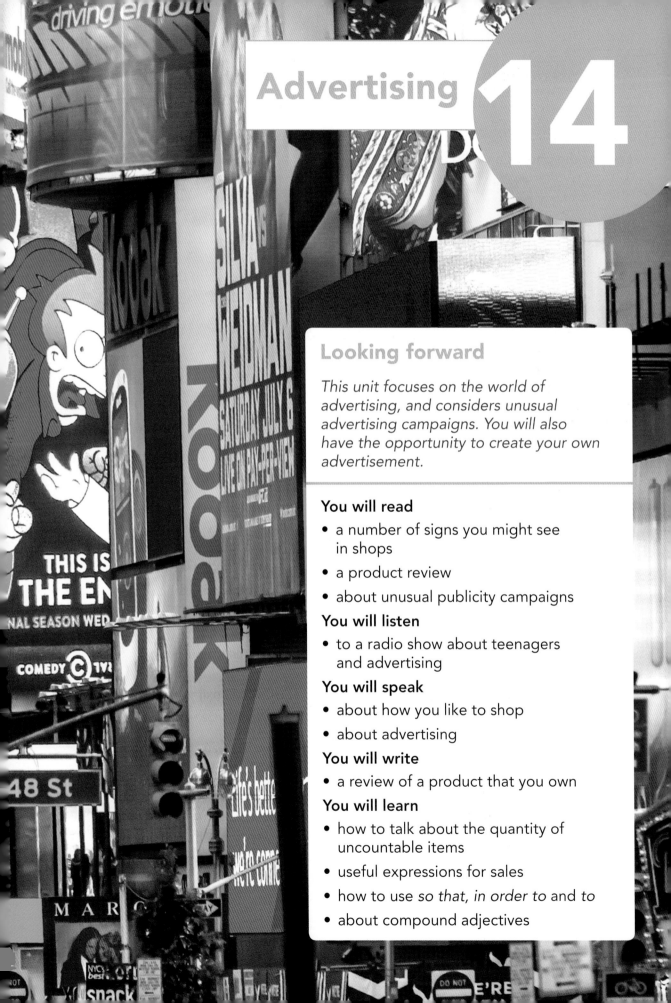

Advertising

14

Looking forward

This unit focuses on the world of advertising, and considers unusual advertising campaigns. You will also have the opportunity to create your own advertisement.

You will read
- a number of signs you might see in shops
- a product review
- about unusual publicity campaigns

You will listen
- to a radio show about teenagers and advertising

You will speak
- about how you like to shop
- about advertising

You will write
- a review of a product that you own

You will learn
- how to talk about the quantity of uncountable items
- useful expressions for sales
- how to use *so that*, *in order to* and *to*
- about compound adjectives

It's on sale!

Look at the photos and discuss.

A

B

- When it comes to shopping, are you more like the person in picture A or B? Explain your answer.
- What shops do you usually go to and what types of things do you usually buy?
- Are you careful with your money? Do you look carefully at prices when you are shopping?
- Do you compare prices between different shops before you buy things? Why? / Why not?
- Do you usually buy expensive items when they are on sale? Why? / Why not?

Reading: special offers!

1 **Read the signs quickly and match them to the shops where you might see them.**

a bag shop   a supermarket   a clothes shop   a café   a furniture shop

2 **Read again and choose the correct options.**

1

> **Special offer. Today only!**
>
> **Come in out of the cold and enjoy a special treat: a slice of freshly baked cake with a cup of coffee only $1.99.**

This offer is:
a just for coffee
b just for cake
c for coffee and cake.

2

> Amazing discounts on hundreds of pieces of furniture!
>
> All sofas down by 10%. Up to 20% off beds.
>
> See in store today! Limited time only, while stocks last.

This sale:
a is always on at this store
b isn't going to be on for very much longer
c is going to go on for at least one month.

3

END OF SEASON SALE NOW ON

Some items of clothing now at half price

Come in and see what we have on display

Unbelievable reductions! Must end soon!

There's a:

a 50% discount on some clothes

b 25% discount on some clothes

c 10% discount on some clothes.

4

FANTASTIC FRIDAY! Many items on sale. Today only.

- all bars of chocolate down by 5%
- all bottles of milk down by 10%
- all cartons of juice down by 15%
- all loaves of bread down by 5%

The biggest reduction is on:

a juice

b milk

c bread.

5

Closing down sale. Everything in stock must go.

Two suitcases for the price of one.

Some handbags down to just $5.

Don't miss out!

This sale is happening because:

a the shop wants to sell old stock so there's room for new stock

b the shop will soon be closed for business

c it's the end of the season.

 Discuss.

- Are there any offers here that would make you stop and go into the shops?
- Which advert or adverts do you think are the best at persuading you to buy, and why?

Vocabulary: sales

Write your own definitions for the words as they are used in the adverts. Use a dictionary to check meanings if you're not sure.

limited   special offer   discount   stock   display
reduction   store   closing down

Language tip

Full sentences are not always used in signs because space is limited, for example: *Must end soon!*

The imperative form is often used because signs are usually trying to get you to do something, for example: *Come in out of the cold! Don't miss out!*

You may also see some extreme adjectives to persuade you to do something, for example: **Amazing** discounts! **Unbelievable** reductions!

Use of English: talking about quantity

1 **What do we do when we want to talk about buying a quantity of uncountable items? For example, how might we answer these questions?**

How much bread do you want?

How much juice should I get?

How much milk do you need?

How much chocolate do you use?

2 **Find eight expressions in the shop signs on pages 154–156 that are used to talk about quantities of uncountable shopping items.**

1   *a ___ of freshly baked cake*

2   *a ___ of coffee*

3   *hundreds of ___ of furniture*

4   *some ___ of clothing*

5   *all ___ of chocolate*

6   *all ___ of milk*

7   *all ___ of juice*

8   *all ___ of bread*

3 **Imagine you are in a shop. Work in pairs to ask and answer the questions from Activity 1 using the expressions from Activity 2.**

Vocabulary: useful expressions for sales

Read the *Language tip*, then copy and complete the expressions used in the signs with the prepositions from the box.

down	for	off	on (× 2)	in (× 2)	at

1   *on* sale

2   ___ store

3   ___ by 10%

4   20% ___ beds

5   ___ half price

6   ___ display

7   ___ stock

8   two ___ the price of one

Language tip

Countable nouns are those that can be counted, for example, *signs* or *supermarkets*.

Uncountable nouns are those that cannot be counted, for example, *bread* or *milk*.

Abstract nouns are always uncountable, for example, *love, happiness* and *fear*.

Spelling tip

Watch your spelling!

One **loaf** *of bread*
Two **loaves** *of bread*

Other words that follow this pattern are: *wolf / wolves, shelf / shelves, scarf / scarves, thief / thieves, leaf / leaves, half / halves.*

Note that not all words follow this pattern, for example, *roofs* and *chiefs*.

Language tip

A lot of sales language is formed with a preposition + a noun or sometimes an adjective. It's easiest to learn these as whole expressions.

Ad break

1 Discuss.

- Where do you see or hear adverts?
- Do you like watching or listening to adverts or do you find them annoying? Explain your answer.
- What's the best advert you've ever seen or heard? Why do you remember it?
- Are there any adverts that annoy you? Why? Would you ever buy this product?

2 (14) **Listen and choose the correct options to complete the description.**

> I heard this really interesting show on the radio today. It was all about ¹[**children / teenagers / middle-aged people**] and advertising. Apparently this market is ²[**not / quite / very**] important to advertisers so they use ³[**the cinema / new technology / newspapers**] to reach people.

3 (14) **Listen again and answer the questions.**

1 What three reasons does Sandra give for explaining why the teen market is so important?
2 Why is the teen market different from the middle-aged market in advertising?
3 How do advertisers make adverts that are specially designed for teens?
4 What advice does Sandra give teenagers?

Language tip

An *advertisement* is information that tries to persuade you to buy something. Short, informal forms are *advert* and *ad*.

Advertising is the business of making adverts.

An *advertising campaign* is a series of advertisements and events to sell a product.

Vocabulary: advertising

Copy and complete the sentences with the words in the box that are taken from the recording.

> influence   focusing on   products   encouraging   taste   developing

1 Sam chooses his clothes well – he's got great ___ .
2 My sister was important in helping me decide what college to go to. She had a big ___ on my choice.
3 We've sold a lot of mobile phones – it's one of our company's most successful ___ .
4 We are still ___ this product – it's not ready yet.
5 My teachers give me a lot of confidence at school – they are always ___ me.
6 We are really ___ making this product as good as we can.

Use of English: *so that, in order to, to*

1 (14)) **Listen again, and copy and complete the sentences.**

1 So advertisers use up-to-date technology ___ get ads to teenagers.

2 Is someone just saying something ___ get me to spend money?

3 I think they can probably give us some advice ___ we don't get ourselves into trouble on the internet!

2 **Look at the examples and choose the correct option to complete the grammar rule.**

We use *so that, in order to* and *to* to say [**why / how / when**] somebody does something.

3 **Copy and complete the sentences with your own ideas.**

● I'm learning English so that I …

● I turned on my computer in order to …

● I opened the window to …

Use of English: compound adjectives

1 **Read the *Language tip*, then match the parts of the compound adjectives that you heard in the radio show.**

1	thousand-	a	aged
2	30-	b	old
3	15-year-	c	second
4	fast-	d	date
5	middle-	e	dollar
6	up-to-	f	changing

> ### Language tip
> A compound adjective is two words that are joined together with a hyphen to make an adjective, for example **well-behaved** *child* and **part-time** *job*.

2 **Make your own sentences using the compound adjectives from Activity 1.**

Speaking: talking about advertising

Work in small groups to discuss these sentences from the radio show. Do you agree or disagree? Explain your answers using the connectives *so that, in order to* and *to*.

● *A good 30-second advert is a good 30-second advert whether it's seen by a 15-year-old boy or a 50-year-old man.*

● *Some advertisers focus on the fact that teenagers want to be cool or fit in or be attractive.*

● *Teenagers are much more likely to buy something they see a friend using rather than something they see in an advert.*

In my opinion, …

I completely agree with …

As far as I'm concerned, …

I totally disagree with …

so that, in order to, to; *compound adjectives; explain and justify point of view in conversation*

1 Read the product review, then number the sections of the review in the correct order.

PRODUCT REVIEW:

Burton X388S mobile phone

★ ★ ★ ★ Very good, but not **outstanding**

I'm writing this review so that I can tell you what I think about my new Burton mobile.

I'm really impressed with the design. This is a very **stylish** phone. Also, it's got a good battery life and music sounds very clear when you play it.

The only downside would have to be the camera, which is a bit **disappointing**. The flash is **unreliable**, so the quality of some of the photos is **poor**.

Overall, I would definitely recommend it to anyone who is looking for an **easy-to-use** phone that offers good value for money.

Writing tip

When you write a *product review*, you share your opinion with other people of something that you have bought and used. You should aim to give a balanced view, talking about the good and bad points. You should decide whether you would recommend this product to others. Remember to use connectives such as *so that, in order to* and *to* in your writing to help you to link your ideas.

CONTENTS OF A REVIEW

___ A sentence to introduce your review.

___ Would you recommend it overall?

___ What do you like about it?

_1_ A short phrase to summarise your opinion

___ What do you not like about it?

2 Look at the expressions in italics in the product review. Which three sections of the plan do these expressions introduce?

3 Look at the adjectives in bold. Which ones are positive and which ones are negative?

4 Choose a product that you own to write a review about.

- Make notes to answer the questions from Activity 1.

- Use the useful expressions from Activity 2.

- Use some of the adjectives from Activity 3.

5 Swap reviews with a partner. Do you want to buy the product that your partner wrote about? Why? / Why not?

Focus on the World

Publicity campaigns from around the world

1 Match the photographs below with the parts of the headlines.

1
NEW SPECIES ...

2
Flash mob ...

3
TURNING TRASH ...

4
... FROM ENGLAND TO FRANCE

a    b    c    d

2 Read the articles quickly. Match the articles (1–4) to the photographs (a–d). Then complete the headlines from Activity 1 with your own ideas.

1

Some people have come up with unusual and interesting ways of raising **awareness** about important **issues**. In South Africa, BirdLife South Africa (a bird **protection** charity) posted a photograph of an unfamiliar bird on their website, with the title 'New species discovered in South Africa'. Within minutes, Facebook was buzzing with people talking about it. It was picked up by other social media sites and also by newspapers. The story got as far as Australia, India, UK and the USA. But the bird in the photograph wasn't real! BirdLife South Africa then posted a video showing how they had digitally changed a photograph of a real bird to create the new picture. The video finished with the simple message: 'If we can get this **passionate** about discovering new species, why can't we get as passionate about losing them?'

2

In the USA, Washed Ashore uses the power of art to focus attention on the problem of pollution in our seas and oceans. Artists have created giant sculptures, including a sea turtle called Herman and an octopus called Octavia. These creatures are made out of rubbish that has been washed onto beaches. It's a **powerful** way of getting people to think about the thousands of sea animals that die each year as a result of our rubbish that ends up in the sea.

3

In the UK, author and comedian David Walliams swam across the English Channel from England to France in order to raise awareness of the charity work of Sport Relief. This 34 km swim is described as one of the hardest **challenges** on the planet, and fewer than 10% of people who have tried to do it have **succeeded**. But he did it in only 10 hours and 34 minutes, and raised over £1 million for charity.

4

In China, the traffic police used the power of music and dance to get their important message across about road safety. On National Road Safety Day, hundreds of young people joined traffic police in a square in the city of Chongqing. They danced together under red signs that gave road **safety** information to drivers and pedestrians. Organisers believe that young people especially learned a lot from the event.

Did you know …?

A *flash mob* is when a group of people suddenly get together in a public place and do something unusual (usually a dance), then all leave again quickly. It is used to entertain but also to focus attention on issues.

3 **How did people focus attention on important issues? Match the methods to the issues.**

1	the internet	a	raising money for charity
2	art	b	learning about road safety
3	sport	c	protecting endangered bird species
4	music and dance	d	stop polluting our oceans and seas

4 **Match the words in bold in the text to the correct definition.**

1	not being in danger	6	something that stops you from being harmed
2	knowing about something		
3	got the result you wanted	7	having very strong feelings about something
4	something that is difficult to do		
5	very strong	8	important subjects that people are talking about

5 **Discuss.**

1 Why do you think BirdLife South Africa pretended that they had found a new species of bird?

2 Why do you think that Washed Ashore make sculptures of sea animals rather than other things?

3 Why do you think David Walliams did a sporting activity to create a buzz about his issue?

4 Why do you think that Chinese police believe that young people learned the most from their event?

5 Which do you think was the best way of focusing attention on important issues and why?

Project: make your own advertisement

You're going to work in teams to design and make your own advertisement for a new product.

1 **Choose your product.**

Work as a team to decide what product you are going to advertise. Think of your own idea or choose something from the box below.

> a new tablet or phone   some new trainers   a new soft drink
> a new film   a new chocolate bar   a new car   a new restaurant

2 **Research and brainstorm ideas for your product.**

- What are the key selling points of your product?
- What pictures are you going to use?
- What will your slogan be?

> **Language tip**
> A *slogan* is a short expression that is used in an advert. It should be simple and easy to remember and it should summarise the key selling points of the product. Do some research by looking at some real advertisements to get some ideas!

3 **Design and make your advertisement. Make it as eye-catching as possible. Include pictures and a slogan.**

4 **Plan your advertising campaign.**

1 Where will you put this advertisement so that it reaches your target market? Talk about some of the ideas in the box or think of your own.

> newspapers   magazines   online   public places

2 What other sorts of advertising do you think would be useful for your product? Use the ideas in the box or think of your own.

> radio   TV   cinema   social media   a party

5 **Prepare and give a presentation. Work together to explain your plans for the advertising campaign. Answer any follow-up questions.**

6 **Share with the class.**

- Listen to other presentations and ask questions.
- Did you have similar products and adverts or were they all different?
- Which group came up with the most original picture in their advert?
- Which group came up with the best slogan?

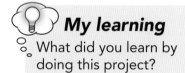
My learning
What did you learn by doing this project?

Review 6

Speaking: looking back

Work in pairs. Look back through Units 13 and 14. Find:

1 a picture of a technological device that you like to use and explain why

2 the name of a social media website you have used and give details

3 the name of a product you might buy and explain why

4 a special offer that you think is good and explain why.

Reading: a quiz

1 Work in pairs. Look at the picture opposite, which is from an article you read. What was the main story? Write down three details about it.

2 Look back at page 145 and check your answers.

3 Look again at the shop signs on pages 154–155 and answer the questions.

  1 What costs only $1.99?

  2 How much discount is there on beds?

  3 What items can you buy for half price now?

  4 What two things are down by 5% in the supermarket?

Listening: what's missing?

1 These are four phrases you can use when you want to check what someone said. Think about how to fill the gaps.

1 Sorry, but I don't f___ you. Could you explain, please?

2 I don't get your p___ .

3 I'm afraid I m___ that. Please could you say it again, a bit louder?

4 What was t___ ?

2 (13B)) Now listen and write down the missing words.

Writing: a product review

1 Write a product review of an item that you use that *isn't* technological, for example, your bike, pencil case or trainers. Look again at page 159 to help you plan your review.

2 Read and edit your review, then show your partner.

Vocabulary: a mixed bag

Work in pairs. Can you name:

1   three verbs to say what you can do on social media websites, for example, *upload*
2   three abstract nouns, for example, *happiness*
3   three words that you might see in shop signs about offers, for example, *50% off*
4   three compound adjectives, for example, *middle-aged*
5   three adjectives you might use in a product review, for example, *outstanding*.

Use of English: talking about regrets

1 **Work in pairs. Say two things that you wish were different about the present.**

> I wish I ...   If only I ...

2 **Say two things that you regret about the past.**

> I should have ...   I shouldn't have ...

Use of English: multi-word verbs and *so that, in order to* and *to*

1 **Work in pairs, Student A and Student B. Complete the tasks in your box.**

Student A

Rewrite the sentences, replacing the words in bold with *give* + preposition.

1   Paul **stopped** using his laptop for a week.
2   This lady is **letting people have free** books!
3   The teacher **gave** the homework to **all the students**.

Write one sentence instead of two, using *so that, in order to* or *to*.

4   I am going to the shops. I want to buy a newspaper.
5   Liam phoned Tarun. He invited him to his party.
6   Graham went online. He bought some cinema tickets.

Student B

Rewrite the sentences, replacing the words in bold with *give* + preposition.

1   Maria **returned** my tablet.
2   My dad finally **agreed** and let me use his computer.
3   I **gave** my homework **to my teacher** this morning.

Write one sentence instead of two, using *so that, in order to* or *to*.

4   Sara left at six o'clock. She caught the early train to work.
5   Oliver is saving money. He wants to buy a tablet.
6   Yasmin opened the door. She let the cat out.

---

2 Swap notebooks. Read and correct each other's sentences.

3 Check your answers with your teacher. You get one point for each correct sentence.

Great inventors

15

Looking forward

The unit considers some exciting inventions created by teenagers, and gives you the opportunity to think about the world's best and worst inventions.

You will read
- an article about teenage inventors
- about infectious diseases

You will listen
- to a podcast about important inventions

You will speak
- about the best and the worst inventions

You will write
- a story about an invention
- cards for an inventions timeline

You will learn
- how to use relative clauses with prepositions
- which verbs take the *–ing* form and which verbs take *to* + verb
- the present perfect continuous

Young inventors

Reading: young inventors and their great ideas

1 **Look at the photos and discuss.**

a
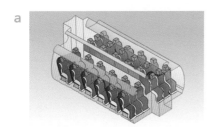

b

c
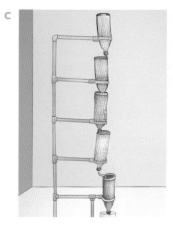

- Guess the use of each of these inventions.
- Which ones do you think were invented by teenage inventors and why?

2 **Read the article quickly and match the pictures (a–c) above with the uses (1–3).**

1 a way of keeping medicines cool when they are being transported without ice or electricity

2 a way of cleaning water using corn cobs

3 a way to stop germs from spreading on planes

Language tip
If you *invent* something you are the first person to think of something or to make it. The item you invent is called an *invention*. The person who makes the invention is called an *inventor*.

TEENAGE INVENTORS

Some of the most exciting inventions of recent years have come from the minds of teenagers.

Raymond Wang from Canada was only 17 years old when he invented a new way to stop germs from spreading in aeroplanes. His invention, for which he won the world's top school science competition, changes the way in which air moves inside an aeroplane. It creates virtual walls of air around each person. This invention only costs $1000 to install on an aeroplane, and could be very important in the future to stop serious diseases from spreading.

Lalita Prasida Sripada Srisai from India has invented a new way of filtering water. She first had the idea when she was just 11 years old. She was walking along a road near her home, from where she could see lots of dried corn cobs. Her invention uses these corn cobs to clean water. The water is filtered through corn cobs a number of times to make it clean. Lalita won a prize for this invention at a science fair last year.

Reading tip
Often, the first sentence of a paragraph is a summary of the rest of it. This is called a topic sentence. Look at the first sentences of paragraphs two and three of this article to see examples. Topic sentences can help readers find information when they are reading an article quickly.

It could make a big difference to many people for whom clean water is not available.

Anurudh Ganesan from India didn't get all his vaccines when he was a baby, and he decided to find a way of keeping vaccines cold while they are being taken from village to village by bicycle. His invention, which he thought of when he was only 15, attaches a bicycle to a plastic cooler in which the vaccines are kept. When someone begins to ride the bike, the plastic cooler is kept cold. There are 19.4 million babies around the world who don't get vaccinated. This invention could save many lives because it will help more babies get the vaccines they need.

> **Reading tip**
> Sometimes writers will communicate messages indirectly. Look for clues that will help you to understand what they are really saying.

3 The writers of these comments have given their opinions indirectly (see *Reading tip*). Read the comments, think about what the writers really mean, and then match to complete the sentences.

Now you've read the article, leave us a comment to tell us which invention you think is the most important!

> It's hard to say which is the most important invention because they are all great. Having said that, I do think that having clean water is the most important issue facing the world today.
>
> *Simone, 14, Australia*

> It's really hard to choose between these inventions. But in my opinion, anything that we can do to protect children from diseases is crucial.
>
> *Ling, 16, China*

> All these inventions are important in their own way. The thing that really worries me, though, is a virus like Covid-19 that spreads around the world quickly and could get out of control. Anything we can do to stop the spread of a virus is a good thing.
>
> *Carlos, 15, Brazil*

1 Simone thinks that ...

2 Ling thinks that ...

3 Carlos thinks that ...

a Raymond's invention is the most important.

b Lalita's invention is the most important.

c Anurudh's invention is the most important.

4 Which do you think is the most important and why? Copy the arrow and rank the inventions from the *least important* to the *most important*.

least important   most important

Vocabulary: useful verbs and nouns

Match the words from the article to the correct definitions.

spread	install	vaccine	filter	germ	attach

1 pass liquid or air through something to remove solid parts such as dirt or dust

2 gradually reach a larger area

3 a substance containing a very small amount of the thing that causes a particular disease, which is given to people to prevent them from getting that disease

4 a very small living thing that can cause a disease

5 put something somewhere so that it is ready to be used

6 connect or fasten something to an object

Use of English: relative clauses with prepositions

1 **Compare and answer.**

*His invention attaches a bicycle to a plastic cooler **in** which the vaccines are kept.*

*His invention attaches a bicycle to a plastic cooler, which the vaccines are kept **in**.*

1 Which two positions can prepositions have in relative clauses?

2 Which position is used in more formal English?

2 **Find three more examples of prepositions before relative pronouns in the article.**

3 **How does the relative pronoun *who* change when there's a preposition in front of it?**

Use of English: verb + –*ing* form or verb + *to* + verb

1 **Copy and complete the sentences from the article with the correct form of the verb.**

1 *She **suggested** ___ (use) these corn cobs.*

2 *He **promised** ___ (find) a way of keeping vaccines cool.*

3 *When the person **begins** ___ (ride) the bike, the plastic cooler is kept cold. This invention could **begin** ___ (save) many lives.*

2 **Look at the examples and match.**

1 Some verbs, for example, *suggest*,   a are followed by *to* + verb.

2 Some verbs, for example, *promise*,   b can be followed by –*ing* form or *to* + verb.

3 Some verbs, for example, *begin*,   c are followed by –*ing* form.

3 **Write three sentences of your own using *suggest*, *promise* and *begin*.**

Talking about inventions

1 (15A) **Listen to the podcast. What question are the three speakers answering?**

2 (15A) **Listen again. Which picture shows the speaker's answer to the question?**

1 John, computer engineer

a    b    c

2 Sam, environmental scientist

a    b    c

3 Tina, doctor

a 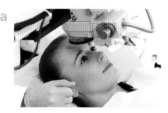   b    c

3 (15A) **Listen again. Why do the speakers think that their items are the most important?**

4 **Rank the inventions in Activity 2 from *most important* to *least*. Explain your answers.**

5 (15B) **The presenter was not listening to the speakers very carefully. Listen to the end of the podcast and find three mistakes in what he says.**

Vocabulary: inventions

Match the words from the podcast to the correct definition.

1	discovery	a	to change something completely
2	potential	b	important or large
3	transform	c	when you learn about something for the first time
4	significant	d	a change over a period of time
5	technology	e	possibility that something could be successful in the future
6	development	f	the way that scientific knowledge is used in a practical way

Use of English: present perfect continuous

1 **Copy and complete the sentences.**

John _____ as a computer engineer for the last 20 years.
Since 2004, I _____ the damaging effect of cars on the environment.

2 **Look at the examples in Activity 1 and answer the questions.**

1   We form the present perfect continuous with *has/have been* +

   a the *-ed* form of the verb.   b the *-ing* form of the verb.

2   We use the present perfect continuous to talk about actions that started and continued in the past

   a and still continue in the present.   b but have now stopped.

3 **Answer the questions.**

1   How long have you been living in your home?

2   How long have you been studying English?

3   How long have you been sitting in this classroom?

Speaking: the best and the worst inventions

1 **Decide which three inventions or discoveries have done the most good and which three the most harm.**

Decide what *you* think. Choose any of the items from the podcast on page 169, the inventions or discoveries in the box below or think of your own ideas.

| television | plastic bag | wheel | guns | electricity |
| fridge | car | aeroplane | radio | nuclear energy |

2 **Work in groups. Discuss your ideas and reach an agreement.**

In my opinion, …	*I believe that …*
I couldn't agree more!	*You're absolutely right!*
That's not always true.	*I don't think so.*

3 **Tell the rest of the class what you chose and why.**

Writing: a story

1 **You're going to write a story, which begins with this sentence:**

"I've got a wonderful idea for a new invention," said Lisa suddenly.

Match the parts of the story (a–c) with the spaces in the plan (1–3). Then answer the questions to write your plan.

a Setting (place)　　b Plot (story)　　c Characters (people)

STORY PLAN
1 _____
Who is Lisa and what is she like? Write key adjectives.
Who else is in your story and what are they like? Write names and key adjectives.
What is the relationship between the people in your story?
2 _____
Where does your story take place?
Are the characters inside? Write key adjectives to describe the room.
Are the characters outside? Write key adjectives to describe the place and weather.
3 _____
Beginning: How does the story start? Will you say what the invention is straight away?
Middle: What happens in the middle? Write down key stages of the story.
End: What happens at the end? Will you finish with a cliffhanger?

2 **Write your story.**

3 **Read and edit your story.**

4 **Swap stories with a partner. Tell him / her three things you like and one suggestion for how to improve the story.**

5 **Think about how you can make your story better and write it again.**

Writing tip

A story needs INTERESTING words – don't use *boring* adjectives, use *exciting* adjectives. Don't use *good*. Use *excellent*, *amazing* or *outstanding*!

Language tip

A *cliffhanger* is an exciting way to end part of a story which makes the reader want to read more. For example:

There was a knock on the door. Somebody was outside …

I looked in the box and I couldn't believe my eyes …

Punctuation tip

Remember to use the correct punctuation for speech. See page 88 for more details.

Focus on Science

Infectious diseases

1 **Discuss.**

- When was the last time you had an infection (for example, a cold or the flu)?

- What symptoms (for example, coughing, sore throat) did you have during the infection?

- How did your body fight the infection?

2 **Read and match the headings (1–4) with the spaces (a–d) in the text.**

1   How are diseases spread?

2   Immunisation

3   Harmful microbes and diseases

4   How do our bodies protect us from harmful microbes?

a _____

We are surrounded by **microbes** (very small living things), and some of them can cause diseases. A disease that can be passed from person to person is called an **infectious** disease.

Type of microbe	Diseases that they cause
virus	cold, flu, measles, chickenpox
bacteria	food poisoning, cholera

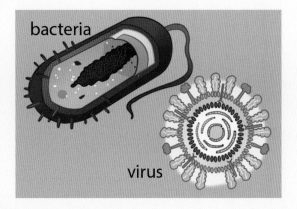

bacteria

virus

b _____

Harmful microbes that cause diseases can be spread:

- in the air
- by animals
- in food and water
- through touch.

c _____

Different parts of our bodies stop microbes from getting inside, for example:

- our skin
- sticky substance in our lungs
- acid in our stomachs
- antibiotics in our tears.

If microbes do get into our bodies, then they are attacked by our **immune system** – the parts of the inside of our body that protect us from harm. White blood cells are important. Some white blood cells kill microbes, and other white blood cells make substances called **antibodies** that stick to microbes, which makes it easier for other white blood cells to kill the microbes.

After microbes have been killed, you will start to feel better. Some of the white blood cells that make the correct antibodies will stay in your body. This means that you won't get ill again, and you will be **immune** to that disease in future.

d _____

This is the way that doctors make us immune to some diseases. It is usually an injection, which is called a **vaccine**. A vaccine contains a dead or weak form of the microbe that causes the disease. Your immune system responds to the vaccine by producing white blood cells with the correct antibody to kill the microbe, so you become immune without getting ill.

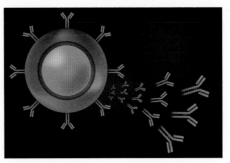

A white blood cell produces antibodies.

Immunisation has been used for centuries. The first modern vaccine was discovered by the British doctor Edward Jenner in 1796. Since then, immunisation has been very successful in completely destroying some diseases and in preventing lots of deaths from other diseases.

3 **Match the words in bold in the text to the definitions.**

1   parts of the body that protect it from harmful microbes
2   a very small amount of the thing that causes a disease, which is given to people to stop them from getting it
3   very small living things
4   two types of harmful microbes
5   a word to describe a disease that can be spread from person to person
6   substances produced by white blood cells that stick to harmful microbes
7   safe from being affected by a particular disease
8   making a person immune to infection with a vaccine

4 **Explain how these things happen.**

1   the ways that an infectious disease can be spread
2   how a sneeze can spread disease
3   the ways that microbes are stopped from entering our bodies
4   how our immune system attacks harmful microbes
5   why we become immune to diseases after we've had them once
6   how a vaccine makes us immune

Did you know...?
Have you ever heard the old saying: *coughs and sneezes spread diseases!* This is a fact. Tiny drops of water carrying the microbe can travel a long way in the air when you cough or sneeze. Then the microbe is breathed in by another person and they become infected.

5 **Discuss.**

1   Next time you have a cold, what will your immune system be doing inside your body?
2   What was the most interesting thing that you learned today?

Project: make an inventions timeline

You're going to make your own timeline of inventions and discoveries.

1 **Make four invention or discovery cards.**

- Choose four inventions or discoveries.
- For each, find out the inventor and the year it was invented or discovered.
- Make four cards. Include photographs or pictures if you want to. On one side (face up) write the invention and the name of the inventor. On the other side (face down) write the invention, the name of the inventor, and the year it was invented.

For example:

Face up

Face down

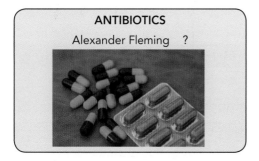

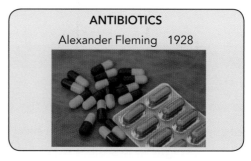

Face up

Face down

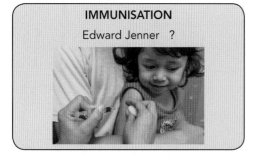

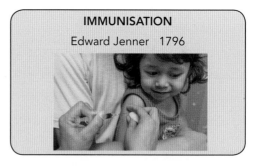

2 **Work in groups of four or five and make a timeline.**

- Mix all your cards together and lay them all out face up so that you can't see the years.
- Discuss when you think these inventions were invented, from earliest to the most recent.
- Put the cards in a timeline that you all agree on.
- Turn the cards over and see if you were correct.

3 **Discuss with the class.**

- Who came up with the most unusual invention?
- Which invention was the oldest?
- Which invention was the most modern?

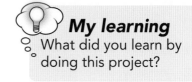

My learning
What did you learn by doing this project?

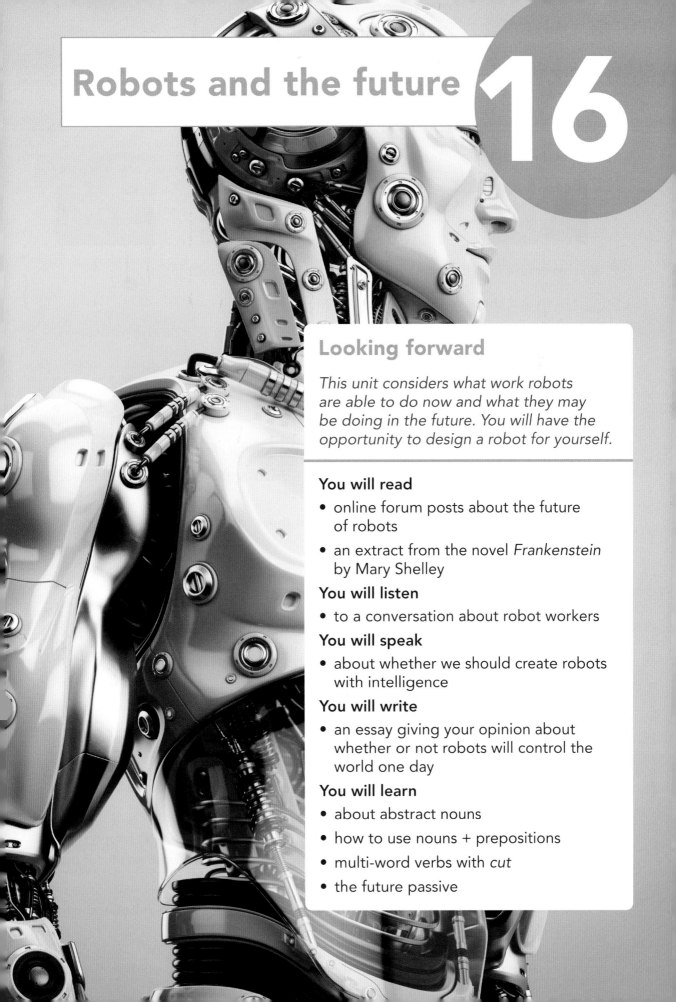

Robots and the future

16

Looking forward

This unit considers what work robots are able to do now and what they may be doing in the future. You will have the opportunity to design a robot for yourself.

You will read
- online forum posts about the future of robots
- an extract from the novel *Frankenstein* by Mary Shelley

You will listen
- to a conversation about robot workers

You will speak
- about whether we should create robots with intelligence

You will write
- an essay giving your opinion about whether or not robots will control the world one day

You will learn
- about abstract nouns
- how to use nouns + prepositions
- multi-word verbs with *cut*
- the future passive

Robot workers

Listening: jobs that robots can do

1 Look and match the photos to the words. | pharmacist   farmer   journalist   surgeon

1    2    3    4

2 Which of these jobs do you think can now be done by robots?

3 (16A) Listen and check your answer to Activity 2.

4 (16A) Listen again and answer the questions.

1 What job does Ahmed want to do when he grows up?
2 What subjects can robot journalists write stories about?
3 What jobs can robot farmers do on farms?
4 Where does the robot pharmacist work?
5 How many mistakes did the robot pharmacist make in its first 350 000 jobs?

> ### Listening tip
> People don't always say exactly what they mean. Think carefully about the context to help you understand what they really want to say.

5 (16A) Listen again. Note one advantage and one disadvantage of getting robot workers to do each of these four jobs. Discuss in pairs.

6 (16A) Read the *Listening tip* and listen. Which of these ideas does Laurence communicate without using the exact words?

1 Robots are more efficient than humans when it comes to studying information.
2 It's cheaper for a farmer to use machines to do farm work rather than people.
3 It's hard for farmers to find enough people to do all the work on a farm.
4 A robot pharmacist doesn't make as many mistakes as a human pharmacist.
5 The work of a robot surgeon is more precise than a human surgeon.
6 Robots will never be able to do all the work that humans can.

Vocabulary: useful adjectives

1 (16A) Listen again to how these adjectives are used in context and match to the correct definitions.

| efficient   creative   cost-effective   reliable   exact   impossible |

1 good at having new ideas
2 accurate in all details
3 able to do tasks successfully, without wasting time or energy
4 that you can trust to work well
5 unable to be done or happen
6 producing the best results for the amount of money spent

2 Which of the adjectives from Activity 1 would you use to describe a robot and why?

Use of English: nouns + prepositions

1 (16A) **Match the two halves of the sentences from the recording, then listen to check your answers.**

1   I've always had an **interest**
2   They write **stories**
3   One **disadvantage**
4   One **advantage**
5   They might not have the correct **reaction**

a   **about** them.
b   **of** a robot pharmacist is that it's very reliable.
c   **to** a problem.
d   **in** writing.
e   **of** robot journalists is that they aren't very creative.

2 **Make your own sentences using the nouns + prepositions in bold in Activity 1.**

Speaking: intonation of tag questions

1 (16A) **Copy and complete the sentences that you heard in the recording with the correct tags. Then listen to check your answers.**

1   *You wanted to be a journalist at one time, ___?*
2   *But a robot can't be a journalist, ___?*
3   *But farmers still pay a lot of money to keep the machines running properly, ___?*

2 **Look at the examples in Activity 1 and choose the correct options.**

1   A positive statement is followed by a:
   a   positive tag   b   negative tag.
2   A negative statement is followed by a:
   a   positive tag   b   negative tag.

3 (16B) **We can use rising or falling intonation with tag questions. You will hear each sentence twice, the first time with rising intonation and the second time with falling intonation. Listen and complete the sentences.**

We use tag questions with:

1   ___ intonation when we aren't sure of something and want to find out. It's like a real question.
2   ___ intonation when we know something but we just want the listener to agree with us. It's not a real question.

4 (16B) **Listen again and repeat.**

5 **Say three sentences of your own with tag questions.**

Robots of the future

1 **Discuss.**

> *Who knows what robots will be able to do in 20 or 50 years from now?*

- What do you think robots will be able to do in 50 years?
- How do you think that they will have a positive influence on our lives in the future?
- Can you think of any ways that they might have a negative influence on our lives in the future?

2 **Read quickly and answer the questions.**

1 Which two people think that robots will have a positive influence in the future?
2 Which two people think that robots will have a negative influence in the future?

Robots are becoming more and more important in many areas of our lives. But what does the future hold? Will robots continue to make our lives easier? Or is there a danger that we will be replaced by robots one day? We asked some people for their opinions.

What is the future ROLE of ROBOTS?

 Robots have an important **role** in our car factory – they lift heavy items, cut out shapes, cut up parts and join parts together. They are efficient, reliable, exact and cost-effective. If we didn't have them, our delivery of new cars to our customers would be cut off. What's more, robots are improving every day. From next year, robots are going to be used to do more and more jobs in our factory. I don't see a problem with this – most of the time they simply do the job better than we can!

Tim, manager, car factory

I'm worried because robots are doing more and more of our jobs, so we are cutting down the number of jobs that are available for people to do. Some people think that by the 2030s, 40% of all jobs will be done by robots. This will lead to a lot of **unemployment** around the world. What will happen to all those people whose **employment** is lost?

Paula, office manager

I think that robots are going to become even more important in the future. They will do all the boring jobs that humans don't want to do. This is an exciting **opportunity** because we can spend our time doing more interesting jobs. I also heard that robots are going to be sent to explore even deeper into space in the next few years. I wonder what's going to be found out there …

Mina, computer engineer

There's an important moral question here: should we continue to make robots that are more and more intelligent? Personally, I strongly believe that's morally wrong and I'm nervous about where it will lead. There will come a point when robots will have more **intelligence** than humans. When that happens, there's a real **risk** that we will be controlled by robots.

Evan, scientist

3 Answer the questions.

1 Why isn't Tim worried about robots doing our jobs for us?

2 Why does Paula disagree with the idea that robots should do more jobs for us?

3 Why does Mina think it will be good for humans if robots do more of our boring jobs?

4 Why is Evan nervous about the development of robots?

Vocabulary: abstract nouns

Copy and complete the sentences with the words in bold in the article.

1 If you have a ___ in something, you have a specific part to play in a situation.

2 ___ is a situation where people want to work, but they can't find jobs because there aren't enough of them.

3 ___ is work that you are paid to do.

4 If you have an ___ , it means that you can do something that you want to do.

5 A person who understands and learns things quickly and well has ___ .

6 If something is a ___ , then there's a possibility that something bad will happen as a result of it.

Vocabulary: multi-word verbs with *cut*

1 Find four multi-word verbs in the article with *cut* + preposition.

2 Match the multi-word verbs from Activity 1 to the correct definition.

1 stop providing

2 cut the shape of something from something bigger

3 reduce

4 cut into smaller pieces

3 Write sentences of your own using the multi-word verbs.

Use of English: future passive

1 Copy and complete these two sentences from the article.

1 *Or is there a danger that we ___ by robots one day?*

2 *From next year, robots ___ to do more and more jobs in our factory.*

2 Look again at the article and find two more examples of a *will* future passive and two more examples of a *be going to* future passive.

3 Answer the questions.

1 How do we form the future passive with *will* and when do we use it?

2 How do we form the future passive with *going to* and when do we use it?

3 What preposition do we use in the passive when we want to say who or what has done the action of the verb?

4 Write these sentences in the passive. Only use *by* if necessary.

1 I think that thousands of people will use this robot.

2 People aren't going to clean the house tomorrow.

3 Will someone fix the robot?

4 Someone is going to deliver the package this afternoon.

5 Leonardo's and Sons won't employ robots.

6 Are the people going to open the restaurant tonight?

> ### Spelling tip
>
> When a verb ends in a vowel + *l*, we double the *l* before adding *–ed* to make the past participle in British English, for example:
>
> *control – controlled*
>
> *travel – travelled*
>
> *equal – equalled*

Speaking: a moral question

> *There's an important moral question here: should we continue to make robots that are more and more intelligent?*

A
> *Personally, I strongly believe that's morally wrong and I'm nervous about where it will lead. There will come a point when robots will have more intelligence than humans. When that happens, there's a real risk that we will be controlled by robots.*

B
> *Well, if you ask me, we should try to make robots as intelligent as possible, so that they can do more jobs for us. They will never be more intelligent than we are and they will never control us.*

1. **Do you agree with A or B? Take a class vote.**

2. **Discuss in groups. Use some of the useful expressions in the box.**

3. **Take another class vote. Has anyone changed their minds after the discussion?**

Useful expressions for discussions

To give your opinion:

I strongly believe …   *Well, if you ask me, …*

To agree with what someone has said:

That's just what I was thinking!   *I couldn't agree with you more.*

To disagree with what someone has said:

I'm afraid I disagree.   *I'm not sure about that.*

Writing: an opinion essay

1. **You're going to write an essay: *Robots will control the world one day. Do you agree?* Write a plan.**

Introduction	State your opinion	*In my opinion, …*
Paragraph 1	Reason 1	*First, …*
Paragraph 2	Reason 2	*Also, …*
Paragraph 3	Reason 3	*What is more, …*
Conclusion	Final thought	*In conclusion, …*

2. **Write your essay. Use your essay plan and the useful expressions for starting paragraphs.**

3. **Read and edit your essay. Check:**
   - Have I got an introduction and conclusion?
   - Have I included some good ideas in different paragraphs?
   - Have I used the correct punctuation?
   - Are the words spelled correctly? Check any that you aren't sure about.

4. **Swap essays with someone who has a different opinion from you. Tell them which of their arguments you liked best.**

Focus on Literature

Creating excitement in a story

Frankenstein was written by Mary Shelley In 1818. The main character, Dr Frankenstein, is a scientist who tries to make a human and bring it to life.

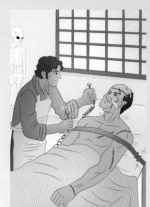

1 Discuss.

- Have you heard of the book, Frankenstein? What do you know about it?

2 Read the text quickly and choose the best sentence to describe what is happening.

a Dr Frankenstein achieves his aim in bringing the creature to life.

b Dr Frankenstein tries but fails to bring the creature to life.

c Dr Frankenstein decides not to try to bring the creature to life.

It was on a dark November night that I was finally successful in my work. I was very worried as I got all my equipment together in the **laboratory**. Would I be able to bring the lifeless thing at my feet to life? It was already one o'clock in the morning and rain was falling on the windows. My candle had almost gone out when I saw the yellow eye of the **creature** open. He breathed hard and his body moved suddenly. He was **alive**!

How can I describe how I felt when this happened? How can I describe the creature that I had spent so long making? I had chosen beautiful, black hair and white teeth for my creature. But these things just made his watery eyes, dried-up skin and straight black lips look even more horrible.

I had worked for nearly two years to make this creature. I wanted it more than anything. But now, horror and **disgust** filled my heart when I looked at what I had made.

I hurried out of the laboratory and fell into bed. I slept because I was so tired, but I had strange and frightening dreams. I woke up suddenly in horror. By the light of the yellow moon, I could see the creature – the miserable thing that I had made. His eyes, if you can call them eyes, were looking at me. His mouth opened and he made some strange noises, which I couldn't understand. He had a smile on his face. He reached out his hand as if he wanted to hold onto me, but I escaped and ran downstairs.

I hid in the garden and stayed there for the rest of the night, walking up and down **nervously**. I listened carefully and jumped at the smallest sound. I was afraid that the creature might come back.

No man could stand to look at the horrible creature I had made. I spent the night unhappily and fell on the ground **exhausted**. I felt so disappointed. All my dreams had now become a **nightmare**.

The next morning, I went for a walk. The rain was pouring down from a black sky. I was shaking. I couldn't think or talk about what I had done the night before. I decided to go home and walked back quickly.

> I was afraid that the creature might still be in my bedroom. I ran upstairs and stopped outside the door. I was cold and I **shivered**. I pushed the door open quickly. But there was nothing there. I stepped inside. The room was empty. Had it all been a dream or had the creature run away?

3 Read again and number the parts of the story (a–f) in the correct order.

a Dr Frankenstein looks at the creature and is frightened.

b The creature reaches out to the doctor in his dream.

c The doctor returns to his house and goes to his bedroom, which is empty.

d The creature comes to life.

e In the morning, the doctor goes for a walk.

f The doctor runs away into the garden and spends the night there.

4 Mary Shelley is very good at creating excitement in her story. Read the tips and find examples of where she does each of these things in her text.

Writing an exciting story

1 Use questions that don't need answers.

2 Use a mixture of long and short sentences.

3 Use short paragraphs.

4 Use powerful adjectives to bring things to life and powerful verbs to create movement.

5 Put characters in dangerous situations.

6 Show the feelings of characters.

5 Match the words in bold in the text with the correct definition.

1 a living thing that is not a plant

2 a building or room where scientific work is done

3 a very strong feeling of not liking something

4 a bad dream

5 shaking because you were cold, frightened or sick

6 very tired

7 living, not dead

8 in a frightened or worried way

6 Discuss.

- What do you think is going to happen next in the story? What will Dr Frankenstein do? What will the creature do? How do you think the book will end?

- Dr Frankenstein wanted to make a person. Do you think this is morally right or wrong? Explain your answers.

Project: design a new robot

You're going to design a robot in groups, make a poster about it and present your ideas to the rest of the class.

1 **Brainstorm ideas for your robot.**

- What will your robot be able to do? Why?

- How will it be useful in your life or the lives of others?

- What will it look like? Will it be large or small? Why?

- Will it move? If yes, how will it move?

- How will it be controlled?

- What will it be made of?

- Who will buy it and how much will it cost?

- Will you give it a name?

- How intelligent will you make your robot and why?

2 **Select your best ideas and make the poster.**

- Draw a rough design of what your robot will look like.

- Highlight and explain what each part of the robot will be used for.

- Include any other interesting information about it.

3 **Prepare and give a presentation. Work together to talk about the choices you have made about your robot. Answer any follow-up questions.**

4 **Listen to other groups and ask questions.**

5 **Share with the class.**

- Which robot was the most useful?

- Which robot had the best design?

- Which robot was the most unusual?

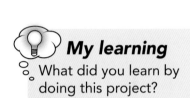

My learning

What did you learn by doing this project?

End-of-year review

Work in pairs. Look back over Units 9–16 and decide.

1 Which unit topic did you like best and why?

2 Which text that you read was the most interesting and why?

3 Which conversation, radio show or podcast that you listened to was the most interesting and why?

4 Which topic of discussion did you have the strongest opinions about and why?

5 Which of the texts that you wrote did you think was the most interesting and why? Which did you find the hardest? Which did you find the easiest? Why?

Vocabulary: what's the word?

1 **Work in groups. Choose five new words that you learned in Units 9–16 and make word cards. Write the first letter of the word and a clue on one side of a piece of the card and the answer on the other side, for example:**

v ....: a weak or dead form of a disease, which is given to people to prevent them from getting it	vaccine

2 **Swap cards with another group.**

3 **Put the cards in a pile with the answers on the bottom. Take it in turns to take a card and guess the word.**

Use of English: multi-word verbs

1 **Work in pairs. Your teacher will give you one of the four lists of multi-word verbs. Write a sentence using each verb to show its meaning.**

A	B	C	D
give up	give back	give in	give something in
give away	give out	put through	put down
put on	put out	put away	put off
cut off	cut out	cut down	cut up

2 **Work with another pair who wrote sentences for the same list. Compare your sentences. Decide which is the best example sentence for each verb.**

3 **Work in a different group of four. (All of you will have looked at verbs from different lists.) Teach each other the meaning of the verbs and read out your example sentences.**

These four students want to do some work experience. Below are six small adverts for places that are looking for students to do work experience. Choose the best place for each person.

Juliana is very creative and she loves writing and painting. She also enjoys cycling in her free time. She writes a blog every month about her hobbies. She is very reliable – she always does her homework and never hands it in late.

Some people might say that Dan is addicted to his computer. But this does mean that he is very knowledgeable about technological devices. He's got his own website and is even working on his own app! He also plays basketball, but prefers to work on his computer.

Ricardo is extremely kind and helpful, and has volunteered at a local charity for the last three months. He helps disabled children to read books and play games. He loves science and wants to study to be a doctor in the future.

Denita plays several instruments and loves performing in her school concerts. She dreams about a career as a musician. She has a lot of friends and enjoys spending time with them at weekends. Sometimes, she cooks dinner for everyone!

Hospital Helpers

We're looking for reliable young people to do work experience at the local hospital during the summer months. This is a great opportunity for anyone who is considering a career as a doctor. You will work in the hospital offices, but you will also get to see doctors at work. Send us an email if you are interested telling us why you think you are right for this job.

Sports Seven

Open seven days a week, Sports Seven sports centre is looking for volunteers for work experience this summer. You must be confident and fit because this role is sporty! You will help children play football matches and take part in tournaments. If this sounds like a job for you, then send us an email telling us all about your sporting experience.

Gatsby Theatre

Calling all creative students who love music and drama! A small, but successful theatre in the centre of the city, Gatsby is looking for students to do work experience in the summer. You must be reliable and friendly. In this role, you will check tickets and show people to their seats. You will also get the opportunity to meet actors and musicians in the orchestra. Perfect for anyone who wants to study drama or music in the future.

Digital Dream

We are an exciting young company, which makes original computer games and easy-to-use apps for mobile phones. We are always looking out for young people who love computers – some of our best games were designed by teenagers! If this sounds like you, then send us a message or an email telling us why you want to work in the digital world.

Daily View

Are you good at thinking up new ideas? Do you like talking to people and writing about your experiences? If your answer to these questions is yes, then you should think about a career as a journalist. Our newspaper is looking for students to do work experience over the summer holidays. To do this job, you must be full of ideas, but also efficient and able to do your work on time.

City Museum

City Museum is looking for students to do work experience this summer. You must love history and you must love talking to people about history! Perfect for anyone considering a career as an archaeologist. You will work in the museum shop and in the exhibitions. If you are interested, then send us your details!

Writing: a letter

1. Choose one of the work experience roles from *Reading: matching* that you would like to do. Write a letter explaining why you think you would be right for the job.

2. Read and edit your letter, checking your spelling and grammar. Then show it to your partner.

Use of English: rewording

Complete the b sentences so that they mean the same as the a sentences.

Use no more than three words.

1. a Harriet told Emile, "Don't upload the photo!"
    b Harriet told Emile ___ the photo.

2. a "Did you see the art gallery?" Guy asked Pierre.
    b Guy asked Pierre ___ seen the art gallery.

3. a I stopped eating chocolate last month.
    b I gave ___ last month.

4. a There is a possibility that it will rain later.
    b It ___ later.

5. a I regret buying this product.
    b I shouldn't ___ this product.

1 (16D) **Listen to the conversations. Read the questions and choose the best answers.**

1 What did Anne buy at the supermarket?

a    b    c

2 What is Wes going to buy when he has saved enough money?

a    b    c

3 What job does Matine want to do in the future?

a    b    c

2 (16D) **Listen again and answer the questions.**

1 What is Anne going to do tomorrow morning before breakfast?
2 What sort of special offer was there at the shop today?
3 What did Wes's mum give him last month and why?
4 Why can't Wes use a laptop very often?
5 What does Matine think that he isn't brave enough to do?
6 What is he going to do to try to achieve his dream job?

Speaking: expressing your opinion

Work in groups. Discuss by giving your opinion on each topic.

What are the advantages and disadvantages of:

- mobile phones
- living in a city
- supporting a local charity
- buying items when they are on sale
- using robot workers?

Use these phrases to help you:

On the one hand … / On the other hand …

One advantage of … is … / One disadvantage of … is …

One good thing about … is … / One bad thing about … is …

In my opinion, … / As far as I'm concerned, … / In my view, …

Writing: expressing your opinion

1 **Write an essay about one of the topics from** *Speaking: expressing your opinion.* **See page 149 for a writing plan.**

2 **Read and edit your essay. Ask yourself:**

- Did I use paragraphs?
- Did I use the correct punctuation?
- Did I use the correct spellings?
- Did I give at least two good advantages, two good disadvantages and my opinion?

3 **Show your essay to your partner and read your partner's essay.**

- Tell them which of their arguments you think is the best.
- Make one suggestion for how they could improve the essay.

Use of English: correction competition

Read the instructions for the competition. Work in pairs.

- Read the sentences. Four are correct but four are incorrect.
- You get one mark for each correct sentence you find.
- You get two marks for each incorrect sentence that you can correct.
- The winners are the pair with the most points.

1 This is the city when I used to live.
2 Were you expecting to hear this song?
3 Could you pass me that book, please?
4 I've looked all over the house, but I can't find my keys anybody.
5 It's not necessary to help this charity – we don't have to support them.
6 If I had a million dollars, I'll buy a new car.
7 We have been waited since 11 o'clock.
8 The laptop computer will be fixed tomorrow.

Writing: my report

1 **Discuss.**

- What have you enjoyed about learning English this year?
- What have you found easy? What have you found difficult?
- How well do you think you can (a) speak, (b) listen, (c) read and (d) write in English now?
- What do you still want to learn?

2 **Write your own end-of-year report for English language. Write about:**

- what you can do now
- what progress you have made
- what you need to work on next year.

You can give yourself a mark, if you like.

Key word list

UNIT 1

acting
actor
animated film
avoid
character
comedy
director
disappointing
documentary
drama
extraordinary
musical
not mind
plot
realistic
recommended
review
science fiction
script
sequel
setting
special effects
suggest
unoriginal
writer

Focus on Drama

act (n and v)
brave
character
climax
confident
frightened

joking
nervous
scene
shy
silly
stage directions
story arc
wonder

UNIT 2

achievement
admire
argue
athlete
brave
bronze medal
celebrate
championship
cheat
coach (n, person)
competitive
congratulate
gold medal
lazy
match
opponent
professional
referee
respect
silver medal
sulk
tournament
triathlon
unfit

Focus on the World

be allowed to
indoors
invent
original
bounce

Worksheet 2B extension vocabulary

defend / defender
cycle / cyclist
field / fielder
bat / batter
climb / climber
ride / rider
hockey stick
racket
baton
golf club
javelin

UNIT 3

Africa
all aboard
Asia
Bangladesh
board
canal
canoe
China
climate
donkey
energy
India
Indonesia

North America
notebook
opinion
opportunity
path
podcast
printer
region
solar-powered
South Africa
tablet
United States of America

Focus on Social Studies
assembly
fair
free
human right
law
peace, peaceful, peacefully
private
property
speech

UNIT 4
advantage
afford
autobiography
biography
comedy
community
connection
disadvantage
e-books
e-readers
fiction

habit
horror
interview
invention
literature
luxury
non-fiction
professor
report
rescue
romance
rubbish
science fiction

Focus on Literature
hero
imagination
structure
style
truth

UNIT 5
advise
amazed
amazing
blog
blogger
Celsius
condition
spell (n)
disappointed
disappointing
drought
exhausted
exhausting
extreme

Fahrenheit
expect
floods
forecast
heat wave
hurricane
rainfall
sense (n)
severe weather warning
shocked
shocking
simile
terrified
terrifying
thick
warn

Worksheet 5B extension vocabulary
amused
amusing
confused
confusing
depressed
depressing
embarrassed
embarrassing
relaxed
relaxing

Focus on Geography: floods
cause
deforestation
effect
immediate

long-term

refugee camp

response

urbanisation

UNIT 6

about (to mean approximately)

Africa

Antarctica

approximately

Arctic Ocean

around (to mean approximately)

Asia

Atlantic Ocean

Australia

bee

continent

destroy

disappear

disease

enormous

Europe

gigantic

habitat

huge

human

hunt

incredible

Indian Ocean

island

latitude

longitude

magnificent

marvellous

mosquito

North America

ocean

Pacific Ocean

peak

population

rainforest

recycle

rock

South America

species

volcano

Focus on the World

destination

rollercoaster

pyramid

sculpture

carnival

waterfall

UNIT 7

ancient

archaeologist

argue

background

battle

bone

bury

exhibition

farmhouse

guidebook

historian

historical

knight

lie (v)

Middle Ages

mummy

object (n)

period

site

time capsule

tomb

virtual reality

Focus on History

army

dig

emperor

ruins

soldier

statue

UNIT 8

amazed at

anxious about

calm

character

confident

creative

fond of

gender

generous

identical

independent

individual

keen on

media

nationality

personal identity

proud of

separate

similar to

twin

warm

Worksheet 8B extension vocabulary

annoyed with

disappointed with

feel sorry for

responsible for

short of

terrified of

Focus on Literature

continue

copy

imagine

pick

promise

pronounce

UNIT 9

blog

blogger

care about

communicate with

complain about

disagree with

dream about

environmental

issue

pay attention

peace

perform

performer

power

share with

survive

Worksheet 9B extension vocabulary

aim for

approve of

argue with

belong to

concentrate on

succeed in

Music: instrument families in an orchestra

blow into an instrument

brass

cello

clarinet

conductor

cover and uncover the holes of an instrument

cymbal

flute

keep the rhythm

oboe

orchestra

percussion

press the keys

strings

tambourine

trombone

trumpet

tuba

use a bow

viola

woodwind

UNIT 10

appear

architecture

art gallery

benefit

certain

charming

continue

convenient

culture

debate

distance

exhibition

expect

experienced

huge

inexpensive

job opportunities

knowledgeable

likely

lively

local

open spaces

original

peaceful

reliable

shocked

stranger

stress

tiny

topic

transport system

vote

Focus on the World

Austria
Canada
economics
education
Germany
health centres
New Zealand
politics
social freedom
Switzerland

UNIT 11

career
designer
firefighter
lawyer
musician
part-time job
put someone through
put something away
put something down
put something off
put something on
put something out
put something up
put up with something
salary
scientist
survey
tally
training
vet
work experience

Worksheet 11A extension vocabulary

take after
take around
take away
take back

Focus on Maths

add
analyse
calculate
data
divide
mean
median
mode
multiply
range
subtract

UNIT 12

access
against (something in discussions)
care
charity
completely
cruel
disabled
duty
extremely
hardly
in favour of (something in discussions)
involved
kindness

persuade
protect
raise money
rescue
stranger
support a charity
suspended coffee
volunteer

Focus on Literature

blend in
character
courage
friendship
greatness
stand out
strength
wonder
narrator

UNIT 13

addict
addicted
addiction
addictive
comment
device
digital footprint
digital age
Facebook
game console
give away
give back
give in
give out
give up

happiness

Instagram

like

opportunity

post

regret

retweet

sadness

share

smartphone

Snapchat

success

tablet

thought

tweet

Twitter

update

upload

Youtube

Worksheet 13B extension vocabulary

darkness

fairness

kindess

loneliness

sickness

unhappiness

Focus on ICT

click on a link

cyberbullying

identity theft

junk folder

password

personal information

phishing

privacy settings

spam emails

virus

UNIT 14

ad

advert

advertisers

advertising

advertising campaign

carton

close down

develop

disappointing

easy-to-use

encourage

focus on

in stock

in store

influence (n)

item

limited

loaf

on display

outstanding

poor

product

product review

reduction

slogan

special offer

stylish

taste (n)

unreliable

Worksheet 14B extension vocabulary

blue-eyed

brown-haired

good-looking

hand-made

left-handed

long-lasting

middle-aged

old-fashioned

record-breaking

slow-moving

well-dressed

well-known

Focus on the World

awareness

challenge

create a buzz

flash mob

issue

passionate

powerful

protection

publicity campaign

safety

succeed

UNIT 15

appear

attach

cliffhanger

consider

continue

development

discovery

filter

germ

imagine

install

intend

invent

invention

inventor

potential

promise

significant

spread

suggest

technology

transform

vaccine

Focus on Science

antibody

bacteria

immune

immune system

immunisation

infection

infectious

microbe

symptom

vaccine

virus

UNIT 16

cost-effective

creative

efficient

employment

exact

impossible

intelligence

journalist

moral

morally wrong

opportunity

pharmacist

reliable

risk

role

surgeon

unemployment

Worksheet 16B extension vocabulary

bring someone up

bring something up

bring something out

bring something in

bring something back

Focus on Literature

alive

creature

disgust

escape

exhausted

laboratory

nervously

nightmare

shiver

Acknowledgements

The publishers wish to thank the following for permission to reproduce photographs. Every effort has been made to trace copyright holders and to obtain their permission for the use of copyright materials. The publishers will gladly receive any information enabling them to rectify any error or omission at the first opportunity.

Key: t = top, b = bottom, l = left, r = right, c = centre, f = far.

p7 Fabio Pagani/Shutterstock, p8tl kojoku/Shutterstock, p8bl Stokkete/Shutterstock, p8tc Macrovector/Shutterstock, p8bc fivepointsix/Shutterstock, p8tr Esteban De Armas/Shutterstock, p8br Everett Collection/Shutterstock, p11 iQoncept/Shutterstock, p12tl Golubovy/Shutterstock, p12tc Sergey Nivens/Shutterstock, p12tr rwgusev/Shutterstock, p12bl Emiel de Lange/Shutterstock, p12bc Emiel de Lange/Shutterstock, p12br Emiel de Lange/Shutterstock, p13 Monkey Business Images/Shutterstock, p17 DenisProduction.com/Shutterstock, p19 sirtravelalot/Shutterstock, p21l ChiccoDodiFC/Shutterstock, p21cl Brocreative/Shutterstock, p21c Juanan Barros Moreno/Shutterstock, p21cr Pavel1964/Shutterstock, p21r Eugene Onischenko/Shutterstock, p22 kovop58/Shutterstock, p23 Josep Suria/Shutterstock p24tl Jacob Lund/Shutterstock, p24tc Maxisport/Shutterstock, p24tr Sean Nel/Shutterstock, p24bl Nick Walker/Sport Picture Library/Alamy, p24br ShutterOK/Shutterstock., p26 leungchopan/Shutterstock, p27 Bruce Rolff/Shutterstock, p28 razorbeam/Shutterstock, p29 Pepsco Studio/Shutterstock, p30l Jonas Gratzer/LightRocket/Getty Images, p30r Courtesy of Samsung, p32 3DMI/Shutterstock, p33tl Fabio Lamanna/Shutterstock, p33tr neelsky/Shutterstock, p33bl Stuart Monk/Shutterstock, p33br Silviu-Florin Salomia/Shutterstock, p34 Dusan Petkovic/Shutterstock, p36 Jacob_09/Shutterstock, p38 iQoncept/Shutterstock, p39 LanKS/Shutterstock, p40 Billion Photos/Shutterstock, p41 Monkey Business Images/Shutterstock, p42t Voronin76/Shutterstock, p42b WAYHOME studio/Shutterstock, p43 GUILLERMO LEGARIA/AFP/Getty Images, p44 Maxx-Studio/Shutterstock, p46 pathdoc/Shutterstock, p48 Roger Siljander/Shutterstock, p49tl Jonas Gratzer/LightRocket/Getty Images, p49tr Courtesy of Samsung, p49b GUILLERMO LEGARIA/AFP/Getty Images, p50 Rose Carson/Shutterstock, p51 Jhaz Photography/Shutterstock, p52tl Dmitry Kalinovsky/Shutterstock, p52bl Tom Wang/Shutterstock, p52tc joyfull/Shutterstock, p52bc sima/Shutterstock, p52tr zstock/Shutterstock, p52br Lucky Business/Shutterstock, p54l Fesus Robert/Shutterstock, p54c AC Rider/Shutterstock, p54r JACK Photographer/Shutterstock, p55 Rawpixel.com/Shutterstock, p56l Dudarev Mikhail/Shutterstock, p56c Mathee Suwannarak/Shutterstock, p56r AtSkwongPhoto/Shutterstock, p58 Jason Salmon/Shutterstock, p61 ronnybas/Shutterstock, p62l Daniel Prudek/Shutterstock, p62c JaySi/Shutterstock, p62r BlueOrange Studio/Shutterstock, p63 Denis Tabler/Shutterstock, p64 Ammit Jack/Shutterstock, p65 kazhungil/Shutterstock, p66tl blvdone/Shutterstock, p66tc DoubleO/Shutterstock, p66tr Surapol Usanakul/Shutterstock, p66bl Ann Kimmel/Shutterstock, p66bc Alen thien/Shutterstock, p66br Simon Eeman/Shutterstock, p68l kakoki/Shutterstock, p68r zhu difeng/Shutterstock, p69t Mikhail Kolesnikov/Shutterstock, p69c trevor kittelty/Shutterstock, p69bl Maurizio De Mattei/Shutterstock, p69br lazyllama/Shutterstock, p70 canbedone/Shutterstock, p71 Robert Hoetink/Shutterstock, p73 Suzanne Tucker/Shutterstock, p74l FXQuadro/Shutterstock, p74r Andrea Izzotti/Shutterstock, p75l Mooshny/Shutterstock, p75c djumandji/Shutterstock, p75r Mikhail Zahranichny/Shutterstock, p76 Ewais/Shutterstock, p77 Zbynek Burival/Shutterstock, p78 Elnur/Shutterstock, p79 Aris Suwanmalee/Shutterstock, p80tl Georgios Kollidas/Shutterstock, p80tr Ke Wang/Shutterstock, p80bl BAHDANOVICH ALENA/Shutterstock, p80br Maxal Tamor/Shutterstock, p82 Rick Friedman/rickfriedman.com/Corbis/Getty Images, p83 Graphic design/Shutterstock, p86 and p87 GrooveZ/Shutterstock, p88 Andrey Arkusha/Shutterstock, p89 mimagephotography/Shutterstock, p92l Monkey Business Images/Shutterstock, p92r Monkey Business Images/Shutterstock, p93 Vgstockstudio/Shutterstock, p95 PORTRAIT IMAGES ASIA BY NONWARIT/Shutterstock, p97 M-SUR/Shutterstock, p98 Who is Danny/Shutterstock, p99 Zheltyshev/Shutterstock, p100t Steve Hurrell/Redferns/Getty Images, p100b Annabel Staff/Redferns/Getty Images, p101 kwest/Shutterstock, p103 DW labs Incorporated/Shutterstock, p104 Matthias G. Ziegler/Shutterstock, p105 LightField Studios/Shutterstock, p106 Monkey Business Images/Shutterstock, p108 Syda Productions/Shutterstock, p109 KN Studio/Shutterstock, p110t Maciej Bledowski/Shutterstock, p110b stevie_uk/Shutterstock, p112tl aerogondo2/Shutterstock, p112tc Ekaterina Pokrovsky/Shutterstock, p112tr CHAIWATPHOTOS/Shutterstock, p112bl View Apart/Shutterstock, p112bc AnLuNi/Shutterstock, p112br Rawpixel.com/Shutterstock, p113 KN Studio/Shutterstock, p114 christo mitkov christov/Shutterstock, p115 wavebreakmedia/Shutterstock, p116tl byvalet/Shutterstock, p116tc Gr8/Shutterstock, p116tr Pero Mihajlovic/Shutterstock, p116bl AmyPJoy/Shutterstock, p116br Pete Spiro/Shutterstock, p118 Gajus/Shutterstock, p119tl Steve Hurrell/Redferns/Getty Images, p119tr Annabel Staff/Redferns/Getty Images, p119bfl aerogondo2/Shutterstock, p119bl Ekaterina Pokrovsky/Shutterstock, p119bcl CHAIWATPHOTOS/Shutterstock, p119bcr View Apart/Shutterstock, p119br AnLuNi/Shutterstock, p119bfr Rawpixel.com/Shutterstock, p120 Charles TANG/Shutterstock, p121 Rawpixel.com/Shutterstock, p122 Syda Productions/Shutterstock, p123 DW labs incorporated/Shutterstock, p127 Rawpixel.com/Shutterstock, p130 Monkey Business Imagesl/Shutterstock, p131 Little Perfect Stock/Shutterstock, p132 Monkey Business Images/Shutterstock, p134 SpeedKingz/Shutterstock, p135 Antonio Guillem/Shutterstock, p137 Vlue/Shutterstock, p140 kotoffei/Shutterstock, p143 Maria Sbytova/Shutterstock, p145 Antonio Guillem/Shutterstock, p147 Iakov Filimonov/Shutterstock, p150 Rawpixel.com/Shutterstock, p152 enzozo/Shutterstock, p153 Allen.G/Shutterstock, p154l MR.Yanukit/Shutterstock, p154r ptnphoto/Shutterstock, p157 Maksim Kabakou/Shutterstock, p159 Georgejmclittle/Shutterstock, p160l Anthony Devlin/PA Archive/PA Images, p160cl Rafael Ben-Ari/Alamy Stock Photo, p160cr George Ostertag/Alamy Stock Photo, p160r Chris Jobs/Alamy Stock Photo, p162 RAGMA IMAGES/Shutterstock, p163 Antonio Guillem/Shutterstock, p165 Sergey Nivens/Shutterstock, p169tl GaudiLab/Shutterstock, p169tc BARS graphics/Shutterstock, p169tr Preto Perola/Shutterstock, p169cl Tom Wang/Shutterstock, p169c Gyuszko-Photo/Shutterstock, p169cr Stockr/Shutterstock, p169bl Robert Przybysz/Shutterstock, p169bc Ivan Smuk/Shutterstock, p169br Oleksii Fedorenko/Shutterstock, p170l Oleksii Mark/Shutterstock, p170r TWStock/Shutterstock, p172 Andrey_Popov/Shutterstock, p173 Extender_01/Shutterstock, p174tl The26January/Shutterstock, p174tr The26January/Shutterstock, p174bl MAGNIFIER/Shutterstock, p174br MAGNIFIER/Shutterstock, p175 Ociacia/Shutterstock, p176l wellphoto/Shutterstock, p176cl ChaNaWiT/Shutterstock, p176cr kurhan/Shutterstock, p176r Monkey Business Images/Shutterstock, p178tl SasinTipchai/Shutterstock, p178tr Phonlamai Photo/Shutterstock, p178bl PHOTOCREO Michal Bednarek/Shutterstock, p178bc Willyam Bradberry/Shutterstock, p178br RODKARV/Shutterstock, p180t Willyam Bradberry/Shutterstock, p180b YAKOBCHUK VIACHESLAV/Shutterstock, p184 Nestor Rizhniak/Shutterstock, p186t takayuki/Shutterstock, p186ct Djomas/Shutterstock, p186cb MJTH/Shutterstock, p186b Andrey Arkusha/Shutterstock, p189t underverse/Shutterstock, p189b UTBP/Shutterstock, p190 Vjom/Shutterstock

We are grateful to the following for permission to reproduce copyright material:

An extract on pp.14-15 adapted from *Step by Wicked Step* (Play Edition) by Anne Fine. Reproduced by permission of David Higham Associates Ltd; Extracts on pp.46, 47 adapted from *Wisha Wozzariter* by Payal Kapadia, Puffin Books, India, 2012, copyright © Payal Kapadia, 2012. Reproduced by permission of Curtis Brown Ltd and Penguin Random House India; Extracts on pp.90-91 adapted from *I Will Always Write Back* by Caitlin Alifirenka and Martin Ganda with Liz Welch, © 2016 by Caitlin Alifirenka and Martin Ganda, published by Little, Brown and Company. Reprinted by permission of Little, Brown and Company, an imprint of Hachette Book Group, Inc.; and extracts on pp.138-139 adapted from *Wonder* by R. J. Palacio, published by The Bodley Head, copyright © R. J. Palacio, 2012. Reprinted by permission of The Random House Group Limited; and Alfred A. Knopf, an imprint of Random House Children's Books, a division of Penguin Random House LLC. All rights reserved.